# THE TRUST

## LIFE UNDER NEW MANAGEMENT

**HENSLEY**
PUBLISHING

ISBN 1-56322-075-X

**The Trust**

# Table of Contents

# About Photocopying This Book

*This book is dedicated to my wife, Jo Ann, who for twenty-seven years has challenged and inspired me by her faithful example of lifestyle stewardship.*

# Introduction

God wants us to prosper. He really does. Now, before we do anything else, let's look at what that word — prosperous — really means. Any dictionary will tell you to be prosperous means to succeed in an enterprise or activity; to enjoy vigorous and healthy growth; to flourish; to thrive. And yes, it also means to enjoy economic well-being.

Prosperity is a powerful biblical principle. It's a precious promise from God's Word which belongs to every born-again believer in Christ. According to the Bible, being successful, or thriving (prosperity), is God's plan for you. Through his prayer in 3 John 2, the fatherly Apostle John communicates God's heartfelt desire for His children:

> *Beloved, I pray that in all respects you may prosper and be in good health, just as your soul prospers.*

John prayed for the prosperity of Christians. God's Word here is clear. God wants you to succeed and prosper in every area of life. That's good news!

But there is even greater news for those who choose to walk by faith and trust in God's promises for prosperity. Your Creator wants more than for you to be successful and do well in life. Psalm 35:27 reveals the Lord's personal attitude concerning the success and prosperity of His servants:

> *Let them shout for joy and rejoice who favor my vindication; And let them say continually, "The Lord be magnified, Who delights in the prosperity of His servant."*

Yes, prosperity. God delights in the prosperity of His servants. Let me paraphrase the last sentence of this verse for you: "God gets really happy when His kids thrive and do well!" Not only does God want His children to succeed, He is supremely delighted and greatly gratified when they do.

What a tremendous thought! The Creator of the universe, the Holy One who knows the beginning from the end and the end from the beginning, Almighty God Himself experiences extreme personal pleasure and delight when we prosper.

Joy floods the heart of God when His servants succeed. That's awesome!

To be prosperous means to succeed in an enterprise or activity; to enjoy vigorous and healthy growth; to flourish; to thrive.

God delights in the prosperity of His servants.

As an earthly father, I understand to some extent how our Heavenly Father feels about the prosperity of His servants. I have two energetic and creative teenagers living under my roof. The daddy in me frequently (and fervently) prays for a prosperous life for my children. I also make plans and provide specific opportunities for my children to experience success. I am their most enthusiastic, faithful, and loyal fan, who constantly cheers them on to fulfill their God-given potential in every area of life. My teens know Dad is on their side, solidly and permanently in their corner, constantly cheering them on. With all my being, I want them to prosper.

My heart is supremely happy when my children thrive and are successful in their personal lives. Their spiritual growth and personal success bring me great delight. When I see my children succeeding and prospering, there is an unspeakable joy and immensely gratifying satisfaction in dear old Dad's heart. Whenever my children do well, I am the first to stand up, shout, and rejoice! I delight when my children prosper.

God delights in the prosperity of His servants.

But there is more good news about prosperity. In His wisdom, God designed for His servants a simple, straightforward, scriptural plan for achieving prosperity. A promise with a plan. What a good God! Because He loves us, our Heavenly Father has provided us with a plan that encompasses every aspect of our lives. It's called stewardship.

> Because He loves us, our Heavenly Father has provided us with a plan that encompasses every aspect of our lives. It's called stewardship.

Understanding what true prosperity is and achieving it is not hard. There is nothing mystical or mysterious about prosperity. God's light shines brightly on this subject. People, not God, make the principle difficult. We allow doubt and unbelief to complicate this fundamental Bible truth, creating confusion and ultimately the inability to successfully accomplish God's desire and delight for us: Prosperity.

God's plan for prosperity is simple, uncomplicated, and attainable. He has established an easy-to-follow, Biblical pathway to prosperity. Any person who has sincere faith and is willing to obey God and practice the principles in His Word regarding prosperity will succeed.

We achieve biblically balanced prosperity through the lifelong practice of stewardship. Author and speaker John Maxwell once defined stewardship as "the successful management of God-given resources for the glory of God and the good of men." Scripture-based stewardship paves the road to success and prosperity. Paul, writing under the inspiration of the Holy Spirit to the newly-converted Christians at Corinth, forthrightly shares with his fellow believers what their supreme role is as witnesses for Christ in this world.

> *Let a man regard us in this manner, as servants of Christ, and stewards of the mysteries of God. In this case, moreover, it is required of stewards that one be found trustworthy (faithful).*
> — 1 Corinthians 4:1-2

Servants and stewards. That's our job description as Christians. Servant is who we are. Stewardship is what we do. As God's representatives in these last days, our role is clearly defined. We are called, anointed, and equipped to serve and be stewards.

Whom do we serve? First, we serve Jesus. Then, we serve people in His name. In Matthew 20:26-28, the Lord Himself put His personal stamp of approval on servanthood:

> *Whoever wishes to become great among you shall be your servant, and whoever wishes to be first among you shall be your slave; just as the Son of Man did not come to be served, but to serve, and to give His life a ransom for many.*

Jesus was the servant of servants. Our Lord, through personal example, showed us that life is service. Christ's ultimate sacrifice on the Cross was the crowning moment of selfless servanthood. His death for us was the culmination of His stewardship of the holy life and redemptive mission the Father entrusted to Him.

We serve because He served. Following in His steps, we find that servanthood provides the springboard for stewardship. Servants serve best as stewards.

Stewards, in simplest terms, are managers. As Christ's servants, we manage His resources. God entrusts what He owns to us. As God's managers we are charged with the responsibility of reaping a profit and bringing increase to the Kingdom. God blesses His faithful stewards so they can be a blessing to others.

In this study, we will learn about that trust, managing God's resources as a way of life. We'll call it lifestyle stewardship.

Lifestyle stewardship is not only a way of looking at life, it is a way of living. My purpose in writing this study is not to propose empty theory or

Servants and stewards. That's our job description as Christians.

Servant is who we are.

Stewardship is what we do.

discuss pious sounding platitudes concerning stewardship and prosperity. My purpose is to present stewardship as the Bible does: It's a lifestyle for the person on the street.

Anyone who wants to can be a successful steward. Successfully managing God's resources requires a real-life, rubber-meets-the-road approach. Lifestyle stewardship is the daily practice of a scripturally sound philosophy of practical principles which are carried out in the routine of everyday life. Diligently applying biblical management principles in administering God's resources leads to success and prosperity.

My Christian life was revolutionized when I was introduced to the scriptural principles of stewardship. As a new believer in Christ, I heard a preacher say in a sermon that life is stewardship and stewardship is life. I wasn't sure what that meant, but it got my attention. Being a baby Christian who was hungry for God and His Word, I determined to investigate this stewardship stuff for myself.

I must admit, at first I was scripturally naive and illiterate. I had a lot to learn about God's plan for blessing our lives. Having been raised in a welfare household, I grew up believing that I was doomed to poverty; I had adopted a "short end of the stick" mentality. I was certain success was for everyone but me. I thought that if I was lucky, I might escape my surroundings and enjoy a mediocre lifestyle, at best.

I am so grateful for a gracious God who cares enough about us to renew our minds and show us that there is a future and a hope for guys like me. I started on a journey, a personal quest, a spiritual adventure of faith and obedience that ultimately reordered my priorities and rearranged my whole approach to life. The topic of stewardship consumed my thoughts and energy. I got into the Word, and the Word got into me. As I searched and studied, more revelation came. The proverbial "light" turned on in my mind. I discovered that God had a better plan for me than I myself, or any other person, could ever have for me.

His Word said I could succeed in life and prosper!

What I had thought was out of my reach, wasn't. God had a plan for me to prosper!

When I realized that I could be successful and prosperous, I became excited about the possibilities before me. I made a conscious decision to line up my life

Successfully managing God's resources requires a real-life, rubber-meets-the-road approach.

Lifestyle stewardship is the daily practice of a scripturally sound philosophy of practical principles which are carried out in the routine of everyday life.

with the Word of God. I chose to become a faithful and trustworthy manager of God's resources. For nearly three decades, I have committed myself to a practical program of daily management of the vast and varied resources God has entrusted to my care. It has been very personally gratifying.

I am so thankful that my spiritual mentors showed me from the Bible that stewardship is a way of life. It's a faith investment that pays great dividends. I'm happy to report that it really works. My life is blessed. I enjoy a truly prosperous life.

*I discovered that God had a better plan for me than I myself, or any other person, could ever have for me.*

I look forward to sharing with you what I have found. This Bible-based, Christ-centered study will assist you in accomplishing the following goals:

1.  Establishing, and affirming, your faith that prosperity is God's plan for you,

*His Word said I could succeed in life and prosper!*

2.  Convincing you, and confirming, that lifestyle stewardship (managing God's resources as a way of life) is His method for achieving it.

This then is the trust. God bless you richly as we learn about **The Trust** together.

# Lesson 1

## Lifestyle: The Way We Live

*Lay up for yourselves treasures in heaven, where neither moth nor rust destroys, and where thieves do not break in or steal; for where your treasure is, there will your heart be also.*
—Matthew 6:21

### PRINCIPLE
- Our lifestyle reveals our heart.

### PURPOSE
To evaluate our lifestyle in light of God's Word concerning the subject of stewardship. Our lifestyle, the way we live, reveals the true condition of our heart. What we do with what God has given us reflects our priorities. Our lifestyle choices and the resulting consequences affect time and eternity. Our study will reveal how stewardship as a lifestyle is the scriptural way to achieve success.

### DISCUSSION
Success has been defined by some as simply "finding a need and filling it."

A few years ago commercials for a financial investment firm aired on U.S. television. In various scenarios, regular people, just like you and me, were discussing their investments, creating quite a clamor in a lively debate of how to make their money grow.

When a certain investment expert entered the room, talking immediately ceased. The silence was profound as every person focused on this reputable, trustworthy source of investment information. The slogan for the advertising campaign was "When E.F. Hutton speaks, people listen."

I honestly don't know how many viewers really listened when E.F. Hutton spoke. But I am sure it numbered in the tens of thousands. The corporation knew of a deep, heartfelt need people have. The advertisement was a marketing success because someone knew people care very much about their finances. Thoughtfully prepared, skillfully presented, the commercial captured the hearts and minds of success-oriented people everywhere.

Our lifestyle, the way we live, reveals the true condition of our heart.

What we do with what God has given us reflects our priorities.

Our lifestyle choices and the resulting consequences affect time and eternity.

Prosperity-minded people seek success. Responsible people, who want to get ahead in life, are seriously concerned about investing their material resources. Go-getters don't sit on their assets. They take action. They make investments. Their purpose in investing is to make a profit, a positive return on their money. Increase is their goal. Their purpose is to make their money make money. The bottom line is personal prosperity.

People covet good counsel in areas where they lack expertise.

When it comes to success and prosperity, there is an even more reputable, trustworthy advisor than E.F. Hutton. A much higher authority. An everlasting, eternally self-sufficient, experienced, well-seasoned, all-wise expert in the area of investments. He is God. And when God speaks, people should listen.

## Where Your Treasure Is...

Disneyland. Created and built by Walt Disney in 1955, the innovative entertainment concept was ahead of its time. Overnight, Disneyland established itself as the original vacation mecca of southern California.

Some of my family's most memorable vacations have been at Disneyland.

We began visiting Mickey Mouse and his "Magic Kingdom" when my children were very young. Hot summer days; stampeding crowds of children and wide-eyed camera-toting tourists from the four corners of the earth; waiting for rides in lines as long as eternity; aching legs; and all of the rest of the annoyances and inconveniences that go with the "fun" of the Disney experience, pale in comparison to the "magic" of the Magic Kingdom.

Something has always drawn us back to Disneyland. My kids are absolutely convinced that the rides are the magnet that keeps pulling us back. Depending on their age at the time of course, various rides have captured their imagination and affection. My all-time favorite attraction has always been the The Pirates of the Caribbean.

We all know pirates exist for one purpose. Treasure. They plunder people and take their stuff.

The Pirates of the Caribbean is an adventurous boat ride through underground caverns where the subterranean air is a bit musty, the darkness a little spooky. It

Prosperity minded people seek success.

Responsible people, who want to get ahead in life, are seriously concerned about investing their material resources.

Go-getters don't sit on their assets.

gives you a glimpse of the lifestyle of pirates of yesteryear. You witness, at close range, a ship-to-ship gun battle, the shelling and plundering of a seaside town, a raucous, drunken party of the victorious raiders, and the stashing of loot in a treasure room.

At a strategic point in the ride, your boat rounds a bend to reveal a room packed full of glittering jewels, royal crowns, dazzling necklaces, and valuable artifacts. A secret room stacked with treasure chests. Overflowing, jewel-laden containers, pile after pile of gemstones, silver, and gold. How it glitters and glows!

But you can't miss the skeletons. They lie face down in the sand, still and stiff at the feet of their coveted treasure.

The treasure chests are still overflowing with worldly goods—wealth beyond imagination! But the treasure collectors are history.

The pirates of the Caribbean didn't take seriously the words of the Son of God when He warned:

> *Beware, and be on guard against every form of greed; for not even when one has an abundance does his life consist of his possessions.*
> — Luke 12:15

Jesus gives a strong warning. Beware and be on guard. Stay alert in life. Don't go to sleep on your watch. Keep your guard up. Don't get slack and let your defenses down when it comes to coveting material possessions. Fortify yourself against a formidable enemy: greed. Note the Lord says "every form of greed." Dictionaries tell us the word *greed* means excessive or reprehensible acquisitiveness, avarice. In simpler terms, it means to be excessively and eagerly covetous. Absorbed with accumulating. Greedy people set their hearts on accumulating stuff, all kinds of stuff, thinking that stuff will satisfy the longings of their hearts.

There are many ways people can be greedy.

Money, fame, position, power, clothes, and cars are some "forms" of greed in life that we need to constantly be on our guard against. Name others.

_____

_____

_____

Greedy people set their hearts on accumulating stuff, all kinds of stuff, thinking that stuff will satisfy the longings of their hearts.

What forms of greed are particularly tempting to you?

_____

_____

Study Psalm 23:1, 31:19, 68:7-10, Matthew 6:25-33, and Philippians 4:19. What do these scriptures say about trusting God to meet our needs?

_____

_____

According to Ephesians 5:1-3, Colossians 3:5, 1 Timothy 3:3, and Hebrews 13:5, what are some practical ways you can keep your guard up against greed?

_____

_____

*He that is greedy of gain troubles his own house…*
— Proverbs 15:27 KJV

The Bible tells us that greed is not a good thing. The following verses stress why we must be on guard against every form of greed.

> *As the partridge sitteth on eggs, and hatcheth them not; so he that getteth riches, and not by right, shall leave them in the midst of his days, at his end shall be a fool.*
> — Jeremiah 17:11 KJV

*He that loveth silver shall not be satisfied with silver; nor he that loveth abundance with increase; this is also vanity.*
— Ecclesiastes 5:10 KJV

Greed doesn't yield long-term gain. Its appetites can never be satisfied. Jesus says even when you have a lot of possessions, that's not what your life is about. Life is more, far more than being greedy and living a life whose sole goal is to accumulate things. Greedy lifestyles are deceptively shallow and abruptly short-term.

Life is not about how much stuff you have. Possessions are not the proper measure of prosperity. A satisfying, fulfilling life is about stewardship, managing the possessions (stuff) you have for the glory of God and the good of men.

The pirates' coveted treasure was useless. They couldn't enjoy it or share it with anybody else. Their hearts were in the wrong place. They didn't guard against greed. They cared more about stuff than anything else. Their lifestyle was centered on themselves and gratifying their selfish desires. Treasure became their downfall because their hearts weren't right.

# ...There Will Your Heart Be Also

Does God care about treasure? Yes, He does. Differently than pirates, of course! Jesus said, "Where your treasure is, there will your heart be also" (Matthew 6:21). In the context of verses 19-21, the Lord doesn't condemn treasure. Nowhere does He speak against possessing valuable things, whether tangible or intangible. Things and stuff are not evil in and of themselves. Treasure itself is not a problem. Storing it up in the wrong place is.

To keep us from falling into the same sinister trap, Jesus reveals Kingdom principles for properly handling treasure. Study verses 19-21 and answer the following questions.

1. "Lay up for yourselves" is a key phrase in this passage. What does it mean?

   _____

   _____

2. Where are we not to lay up treasures?

   _____

   Why?

   _____

   _____

3. Where are we to lay up treasures for ourselves?

   _____

   For what reason?

   _____

   _____

4. In your own words, what do you think verse 21 means?

   _____

   _____

> Things and stuff are not evil in and of themselves. Treasure itself is not a problem. Storing it up in the wrong place is.

This graphic lesson on God's do's and don'ts is illustrated by the method of contrast. The Lord first gives a "do not." Don't store up stuff on earth. Why? Simple. It won't be there in the end. Something will corrupt it, or someone will steal it. Storing up treasures in this world is futile and vain. A waste of energy and effort. Worldly investments will not last. You can't take it with you. So do not invest your life in this world. Live a lifestyle that extends beyond your earthly existence.

Here, as well as in every instance in the Bible where do's and don'ts are taught, God's "do not" is good for us. He loves us so much that He is not afraid to warn us what not to do.

As a loving Father, for every "do not" in His Word, God gives us a "do." Jesus teaches us to lay up (store) treasure in heaven if we want to make investments whose returns are "out of this world." What we deposit there remains! What is valuable can't be spoiled, corroded, or ripped off! If God is guarding it, nobody is going to take it from us. In glory, our treasure is safe.

In Luke 12:31-34, a parallel passage to Matthew 6:19-21, Jesus gives some important scriptural truths concerning treasure.

> *Seek first His Kingdom, and these things shall be added to you. Do not be afraid, little flock, for your Father has chosen gladly to give you the Kingdom. Sell your possessions and give to charity; make yourselves purses that do not wear out, an unfailing treasure in heaven, where no thief comes near, nor moth destroys. For where your treasure is, there will your heart be also.*

The following five points from these verses are highly inspiring and motivating.

1. Seek God's Kingdom first. He will take care of your every need.
2. Do not be afraid, little sheep. The Good Shepherd is looking out for you.
3. Your Father is glad to give you the Kingdom. Not sad, but glad! Happy to give you the very best blessings His heavenly realm has to offer.
4. Do what I tell you to do. I custom make plans for prosperity for each of My sheep. When I direct you to help others, do it; serve and sacrifice, do it. You will always gain by giving. Focus on storing up "unfailing" treasure in heaven. Nothing harmful touches it there.
5. Here's the point of all this. Keep your heart right and your treasure will be in the right place. If your heart is set on heaven, your treasure will be in heaven. Guaranteed!

Jesus is sending a life-transforming message to His followers. He is telling us to concentrate on the things that will last. Treasure which will last is treasure that comes from hearts that are in sync with God's Word and His will. That's great news for anyone desiring success and prosperity!

Worldly investments will not last. You can't take it with you. So do not invest your life in this world. Live a lifestyle that extends beyond your earthly existence.

What's the key to storing up treasure in heaven? Keeping our hearts in tune with heavenly, not earthly, principles and practices. When it comes to managing resources successfully we must live each day according to God's Word, not the world's ways.

Paul gives Spirit-inspired advice regarding where Christians are to focus their attention and affection.

Keep focused on the things above. Set your mind (something you choose to do) on heavenly things, not earthly things. Look to where Christ is. He is your life. Your reward is with Him. Keep your new heart focused on heaven.

## Stewardship Is a Matter of the Heart

How you choose to manage your God-given resources is a choice you, and you alone, make. What you determine to do with your treasure is decided in the secret chambers of your heart. The following selected passages show how the words *treasure* and *heart* are used together in the New Testament:

Matthew 2:11 _____

Matthew 13:52 _____

Matthew 12:33-35 _____

Luke 6:45 _____

Matthew 6:19-21 _____

Matthew 13:44 _____

Luke 12:33-34 _____

Hebrews 11:26 _____

The overall idea expressed in these verses is that treasure indicates something of value that is stored in a place where it is safe.

Let's take a closer look at what Jesus taught in Matthew 12:33-35 about treasure. Twice in verse 35, the word *treasure* is used as a metaphor about the heart. The setting of this teaching is important. Contrasting a good person and an evil person, Jesus declares that a person is known by his fruit. Good people produce good fruit. Evil people produce evil fruit. Good people do not produce evil fruit; evil people do not produce good fruit. The point of Jesus' sermon is this: A person's words (which originate from the heart, according to verse 34) reveal their true character (fruit). That's a no-brainer!

*If then you have been raised with Christ, keep seeking the things above, where Christ is seated at the right hand of God. Set your mind on the things above, not on the things that are on earth. For you have died and your life is hidden with Christ in God. When Christ, who is our life, is revealed, then you also will be revealed with Him in glory.*

— Colossians 3:1-4

> Good people produce good fruit. Evil people produce evil fruit.

But the religious leaders of the day didn't understand. They were spiritually thick-headed, just plain dense when it came to understanding truth. Blinded by pious, religious pride, they couldn't see their own error. They were bonafide hypocrites. They didn't live what they believed. The self-righteous Pharisees were the epitome of the ages-old accusation hurled at hypocrites in all walks of life: They don't walk what they talk!

The Lord exposed the hypocrisy of the Pharisees. Misguided themselves, they were leading the Jewish people astray with their legalistic, religious-based teaching. They taught the traditions of men instead of the Word of God. Jesus blasted their hypocritical lifestyle with a biblical broadside. Without apology, He boldly pronounced, "You brood of vipers, how can you, being evil, speak what is good? For the mouth speaks out of that which fills the heart" (v. 34).

Go get 'em Jesus! What a pointblank shot to the spiritual midsection! You snakes! (When was the last time you heard someone called a brood of vipers?) Concise, condemning language. How dare you, Mr. Pharisee, think you can speak good when your heart is rotten to the core? Your reptilian mouth speaks only evil, because that is what fills your heart. Rotten heart, rotten words, rotten fruit.

Verse 35 amplifies verse 34. A good man speaks good words out of his good treasure; an evil man brings evil out of his evil treasure. The word used here for *treasure* means a place of safe-keeping. That safe place, the treasury worth guarding and keeping watch over, being diligent to keep it pure, good, and right, is your heart.

Your words and your deeds, which produce the fruit of your lifestyle, flow from your heart.

## Show Me Your Treasure and I Will Show You Your Heart

Jesus cares deeply about our hearts. The state of a person's heart is God's first priority in the plan of salvation. Note that in Matthew 6:21 our hearts and treasures are tied together. To briefly paraphrase, the Lord is saying, "Show me your treasure and I will show you your heart." The way we choose to live our lives is an issue of the heart.

Your lifestyle, the typical way you live your life, flows from your heart. Decisions ultimately made in your head originate in your heart.

Solomon, writing in Proverbs 4:23, strongly exhorts us to be very diligent to watch over the condition of our hearts.

To be diligent means to be steady, earnest, and energetic in application and effort. What a way to live! Diligent people apply themselves in a consistent, painstaking manner to accomplish their desired goals. They keep after it. Souls who are diligent stay on top of what is important to them. The diligent won't be denied, because they value what they believe in. They know what matters to them. They apply themselves in such a way that others also know how much their goals matter to them.

*Watch over your heart with all diligence, for from it flow the springs (sources, issues) of life.*
— Proverbs 4:23

Solomon tells us to keep a watchful eye on our hearts. Why? Because the issues of life (your personal lifestyle) flow from it. The heart dictatet lifestyle.

If your heart is right, your treasure will be right.

## Lifestyle Stewardship: Laying Up Treasure in Heaven

Someone once said that whatever a person loves, that is their god. What do you love most? What do you treasure and value above all things? What really captures your affection? What do you pour your energy and effort into more than anything else? What would you be willing to die for? Tell me what that is, and I will tell you what you love.

If we are not careful, what we love can become a counterfeit God to us.

That's why the Lord Jesus, when taken to task and tested by a lawyer as to what the greatest commandment in the Law was, responded:

> *"'You shall love the Lord your God with all your heart, and with all your soul, and with all your mind'. This is the great and foremost commandment. The second is like it, 'You shall love your neighbor as yourself.' On these two commandments depend the whole Law and the prophets."*
> — Matthew 22:36-40

If we are not careful, what we love can become a counterfeit God to us.

Skillfully maneuvering past the lawyer's trap, Jesus said these two commandments are the greatest commandments in the Kingdom of God. First, love God. Give God first place in your heart. Make God your priority. Love God, and God alone with all your being. That's first and foremost. Top of the priority list.

First things first. Love God.  Second, love your neighbors as you love yourself. Let the love you have received from God flow through you to touch others.

## SUMMARY

Love God; love yourself; and love others. That's what the Kingdom is all about. Every other moral/ethical law and spiritual principle flows from these two. The greatest of all virtues is love.

The lawyer had no rebuttal. There is none. Jesus got it exactly right. God is love. (See 1 John 4:7-21.) Love is the rule of law in God's Kingdom. If you want to be like Him, if you want to be blessed by Him, and be a blessing to others, then walk in love. Love God and love what God loves. Live a life that demonstrates that you love God more than anything else.

We lay up treasure in heaven when we love God, love what He loves, and live our life the way He commands us to live it. That's real treasure, treasure that lasts for this lifetime and the next.

# If You Love Me, Obey Me

Jesus came to earth to show us how to live our lives. In essence, to show us how to fulfill the two great commandments; how to love God, love ourselves and love others. His life pointed the way to a lifestyle that pleases God. Jesus not only talked about love, He walked in love. He modeled a lifestyle of love for us. A practical way of life that reflected God's love in the daily affairs of living.

*Jesus not only talked about love, He walked in love. He modeled a lifestyle of love for us. A practical way of life that reflected God's love in the daily affairs of living.*

The Lord's exemplary life challenges us to go and do as He did. If we are to be like Him, which is the essence of biblical Christianity, we must live like Him — in a lifestyle of love. He loved. We love. Jesus loved through a pre-determined lifestyle. He chose to love and made choices in daily life that reflected that love.

Jesus practiced lifestyle stewardship. Through scriptural management of the resources at His disposal, the Lord's way of life demonstrated that He indeed loved the Father, Himself, and humanity. Jesus Christ preached and practiced stewardship as the pathway to success and prosperity in the Kingdom of God. He, Himself, is our model for lifestyle stewardship. His priorities, His choices, and His actions all reflect a lifestyle of love and obedience to the Father. His lifestyle of stewardship pleased God and blessed man.

All who call themselves Christians are to follow Christ's example of lifestyle stewardship. Jesus made a profoundly simple, yet powerfully insightful statement to the disciples.

> *If you love Me, you will keep My commandments.*
> — John 14:15

The biblical litmus test of the true followers of Christ is this: If you really love Me, as you say you do, you will do what I say and do what I do. Love's truest measure of devotion is obedience.

The Apostle John, called the beloved apostle of love by the early church, certainly understood what Jesus said. Later in his life, he inked these inspired words:

> *This is the love of God, that we keep His commandments; and His commandments are not burdensome.*
> — 1 John 5:3

God's great love for us is seen in the fact that He gave us commandments to follow. His love for us would not allow us to be without direction. He gave us a spiritual/moral roadmap for godly conduct, holy rules for governing the way we live.

We fulfill His love for us and demonstrate our genuine love for Him when we keep those commandments. Take note of what the elder John says about God's rules. His commandments are not hard! Once again, God's commandments are not hard to follow or fulfill! They are not burdensome. God's ways do not put heavy burdens, or weights, upon our spiritual shoulders. Satan's ways and the ways of unregenerate people are indeed heavy, hard, and burdensome. Lawlessness and legalism always produce bondage, misery, and despair. Their unholy and unjust demands make life extremely difficult and burdensome.

God's commandments are not hard to follow or fulfill! They are not burdensome....God's commandments relieve burdens.

But not God's commandments. His ways are neither grievous nor burdensome. God's commandments relieve burdens. The anointing upon His Word breaks yokes of bondage. It's Bible truth. It's easier to serve God than to serve Satan or self. Life is rough and tough when lived outside of God's commandments. Life is brutal and people get down in life when they stray from under the umbrella of God's moral law. Too many of us know how true this is.

God's rules are given for our good. That's true love. And the truth is, His ways are easy to live with when we love the One who gave them.

# Is His Lifestyle Our Lifestyle?

Lifestyle stewardship means living our daily lives as stewards of God, just as Jesus did. If we desire to have the blessing of God in our lives like Jesus did, then we must live the lifestyle He lived.

Last words are powerful words. Just before he died, Joshua made one of the greatest last word and testament statements ever recorded. The complete text of his personal challenge to the children of Israel is found in Joshua chapter 24. After reviewing Israel's spiritual history, Joshua exhorted them to take a good look at the wonderful land God had brought them to and to decide for themselves whom they would serve.

Immense pressures surrounded God's people. Phony gods beckoned their worship. False friends tempted them to indulge in immoral practices. It was decision time. — When push comes to shove, O Israel, whom are you going to serve? Joshua took one last spiritual stand, making his personal deathbed statement that has rung loudly and clearly throughout biblical history. Read once again to his inspiring words:

> Fear the Lord and serve in sincerity and truth; and put away the gods which your fathers served beyond the River and in Egypt, and serve the Lord. And if it is disagreeable in your sight to serve the Lord, choose for yourselves today whom you will serve; whether the gods which your fathers served which were beyond the River, or the gods of the Amorites in whose land you are living; but as for me and my house, we will serve the Lord.

Joshua put the choice of who we will serve exactly where God puts it: on each individual. "You choose" was the challenge. You decide the way you will live. Your lifestyle is up to you. No one else. Here's my choice. This is where I, Joshua, draw a line in the spiritual sand. First, I choose for me. I, Joshua, will always serve the Lord. Whether you choose to or not, I do. Second, I choose to lead my household in the ways of the Lord. They and I, we, will serve the Lord. Our household is committed to serving God and obeying His commandments all the days of our lives.

Bravo, Joshua! He had the "guts" to make a stand — a lifestyle stand. He chose that he and his family would be servants and stewards of the Lord. "Choose for yourselves today whom you will serve" is still valid today. Each of us must take our own stand.

Your lifestyle is up to you. No one else.

"Choose for yourselves today whom you will serve" is still valid today. Each of us must take our own stand.

The choice before you is this: Will you line up your life with the Word of God and practice lifestyle stewardship as Jesus and Joshua did, or will you look to the world, do your own thing, and practice a self-centered way of life? It's your choice.

# Lifestyle Analysis

Before you can adjust the way you live, you must analyze your lifestyle. The following analysis will help you determine whether or not your lifestyle is similar to that of Jesus. First, read 1 Samuel 16:7, which tells us God sees our hearts. Then, respond to the following questions. Use this exercise to line your life up with God's Word.

## PRIORITIES

What you become is determined by what is most important to you. A priority is something you put in superior rank or position to other things. Jesus' priorities were three:

**KINGDOM FIRST**          **LOVE GOD AND MEN**          **SERVE AND GIVE**

Matthew 6:33                    Matthew 22:37-40                   Matthew 20:26

1.  Do your priorities (those things which are most important) reflect Christ's priorities? If so, in what ways?

    _____

    _____

2.  In descending order, list the top five priorities in your life.

    _____

3.  Where do you need to adjust your priorities in light of the Lord's priorities?

    _____

## CHOICES

Decisions determine destiny; consequences follow choices. Life is one long series of choices. You are free to choose the lifestyle you will live.

1.  Do your personal choices concerning how you spend your time, what you do with your money, who you hang out with, and what you do with them reflect the choices Jesus Christ would make? If yes, how are you happy about your choices? If no, what would you like to change?

_____

_____

2.  Name an important lifestyle choice you made recently. How has that personal decision affected you, your family, and friends?

    _____

    _____

3.  List areas you need to improve in your decision making.

    _____

    _____

## ACTIONS

Attitudes dictate actions. The way you choose to live your life is a reflection of what you think and feel about life. What you see is what I be. Actions do indeed speak louder than words.

1.  Do your daily actions, the personal behavior you exhibit, and the way you treat people demonstrate a Christ-like style? If yes, list the ways.

    _____

    _____

2.  What recent action have you taken that exemplify a godly lifestyle?

    _____

    _____

> If other Christians were to look to your life as a role model of Christ-like stewardship, would they have a biblical example to follow?

What recent action didn't exemplifies a godly lifestyle?

_____

_____

3.  Would those who know you best see your lifestyle as Christ-like?

    _____

    _____

If the answer is no, in what areas do you need to adjust your actions?

_____

_____

If other Christians were to look to your life as a role model of Christlike stewardship, would they have a biblical example to follow?

_____

_____

# Lesson 2

## Stewardship 101: He Owns the Cattle

*Every beast of the forest is mine, the cattle on a thousand hills.*
— Psalm 50:10

*The earth is the Lord's, and all it contains, the world, and all those who dwell in it.*
— Psalm 24:1

PRINCIPLE
- God owns everything.

PURPOSE
Our purpose will be to establish the biblical fact that God is the sole owner of all resources in His material universe. As Creator, His signature is on the deed to the earth and all of its inhabitants. Because our Maker owns everything He has made, we have a unique responsibility to Him. God's Word reveals a divine-human partnership in the stewardship process. God owns everything, is senior partner, and gives the orders. Man manages what God owns, is junior partner, and carries out the will of the senior partner.

DISCUSSION
Being the oldest son of six sons raised by a single mom has produced a lifetime of indelible memories. Our household, by virtue of the fact that seven highly individualistic, strong-willed human beings co-existed under the same roof, was constantly, as my mother used to say, "coming and going." There was always something or other going on at our address.

I have fond memories of the places we lived, the houses we called home. For me, there were three: The deep red, white trimmed house on Belt sStreet, where I had an appendicitis attack in the middle of the night. The house on Lindeke Street, at the bottom of a long, steep hill, where authorities blocked off the iced-over thoroughfare with bright yellow barriers after winter snows — and gave my brothers and me some serious sledding time.

Then there was West Rockwell Avenue. We lived there from sixth grade through my high school graduation. It was a simple white house with a large gray porch,

Because our Maker owns everything He has made, we have a unique responsibility to Him. God's Word reveals a divine-human partnership in the stewardship process.

and was surrounded on three sides by a nice sized yard. Each spring I planted petunias in the flower beds and grew vegetables in the backyard garden. The house was not very large, and bunk beds made the upstairs bedroom look like a military barracks.

But the downstairs is what I remember most vividly. The basement was where I shared a room with my brother just younger than me. It was dark. Midnight dark and spooky. Winding, cement steps descended into what seemed like an abyss. A big old coal furnace belched when you walked by. The floor joists overhead creaked. Wind howled through leaky window panes.

The three homes I grew up had one thing in common. They were rental houses. With a limited income, Mom was unable to qualify for a home mortgage. Because we could not afford to own the houses, we leased them. The landlords owned the land and the residence sitting on it. The title was in their name. But our monthly rent payment guaranteed we would have a warm roof over our heads.

Our responsibility to the owner was to pay the rent and keep the property in good condition. We were renter/managers. Mom made sure we took good care of the owner's house. We kept it immaculately clean and orderly. I maintained the lawn. The landlord even hired me one summer to paint the exterior of the house. When major repairs were needed, the owner stepped in to fix his property. We had a positive owner-renter/manager relationship.

I loved the little house on Rockwell Avenue. I cherish memories of passing from boyhood to young adulthood in that wonderful old house! I took great pride in keeping it up for my mom and brothers. But one thing I always knew — it was never ours. It belonged to somebody else. An owner. As renters, we managed another man's property. The title to the house was in another person's name.

> As renters, we managed another man's property. The title to the house was in another person's name.

## The Title Is in His Name

Our society is obsessed with the principle of ownership. People stress themselves out working overtime dreaming of the day when they sign on the dotted line in order to pay obscene interest rates to a financial lender whose only interest is to make money off the borrower's money. And for what purpose? In order to own something.

If I could just own that, then I would be doing great.

Many people mistakenly believe that if they own something, whether it be a house, car, DVD player, stock in a successful company, or some valued material asset, then they will become something. There is a myth in our culture today. It's blatantly untrue, subtly deceptive, and certainly destructive, but a lot of non-thinking people believe it. It goes like this: Non-owners are nobodies. Owners are somebodies.

Ownership, in increasingly larger circles, is synonymous with success.

What do you think motivates people (family background, poverty, societal peer pressure, etc.) to become obsessed with ownership?

_____

_____

_____

List several reasons why people work so hard to own their possessions.

_____

_____

_____

_____

How important is owning things to you? Your family? Your friends?

_____

_____

_____

Share an example of something you wanted to own and how you pursued ownership. Were you happy when you finally "owned" it?

_____

_____

_____

_____

Do you think Christians should strive to own things? Make a list of the pros and cons of ownership.

_____

_____

_____

_____

It's blatantly untrue, subtly deceptive, and certainly destructive, but a lot of non-thinking people believe it. It goes like this: Non-owners are nobodies. Owners are somebodies.

Because I was raised in rental houses, I thought often about owning my own home one day. The idea of ownership appealed to me. It became a life goal. A worthy one. Home ownership is not unreasonable. It's part of the American dream, for goodness sake! There are some very positive benefits to owning a home instead of renting one. But in the light of God's Word, even when our name is on the deed to a house, do we really own it? Are we, in truth, the legal owners? Is it really ours?

I remember well the day my wife and I "closed" on our first home. What an experience! Who could ever forget the stacks of endless legal documents, signing our names over and over again, and the incessant droning of the financial officer's voice as she attempted to explain the infamous fine print. During the process, for a few fleeting moments, I wondered if home ownership was worth the hassle it appeared to be. Finally, and mercifully, we put our signatures on the final papers and received the keys to our new home. What a satisfying moment! I had dreamed of it for nearly four decades. My wife and I joined the ranks of homeowners.

Rejoicing on the drive to our new house, we thanked the Lord for our new residence. As we turned the key in the lock for the first official time, our heavenly Father gently and graciously reminded us that our house was His house. In the natural realm, our names were on the title, but in the Kingdom of God, where things really count, His name was on the title. He was the rightful owner. We counted it a tremendous blessing to become on-site, daily managers of His house.

> As Christians, we belong to God. Everything we have also belongs to Him, because He owns everything.

As Christians, we belong to God. Everything we have also belongs to Him, because He owns everything.

Scripture makes it abundantly clear who owns everything. From the following verses, discover and decide for yourself.

> *The earth is the Lord's, and all it contains, the world and all those who dwell in it.*
> — Psalm 24:1

The earth and all it contains belongs to_____.

To whom do all the inhabitants of the earth (including you and me) belong?

_____

_____

*The heavens are Thine; the earth also is Thine: the world and all it contains, Thou hast founded them.*

— Psalm 89:11

According to this verse, God owns four things. Name them.

a_____ b_____ c_____ d_____

What is the basis for His ownership?

_____

_____

_____

Read Exodus 19:5, Leviticus 25:23, Haggai 2:8, Deuteronomy 32:6, Ezekiel 18:4, and Romans 14:8.

What do these passages have to say about God's ownership?

_____

_____

_____

The above scriptures make a profound revelation: God owns everything! He owns heaven and earth and everything in heaven and earth. Every created being, including man, belongs to Him! You name it, God owns it. His holy name is signed on the bottom line of the universe's ownership papers. The reason is very evident: Everything, all matter, living or non-living, all creatures great and small, were made by Him and for Him. Therefore, they are owned by Him and are accountable to Him.

> Everything, all matter, living or non-living, all creatures great and small, were made by Him and for Him. Therefore, they are owned by Him and are accountable to Him.

"He Owns The Cattle On A Thousand Hills" is a traditional hymn of the church. I remember singing it as a youngster. I can still hear the tune ringing in my mind. It is based on Psalm 50:10: For every beast of the forest is Mine, the cattle on a thousand hills. The message of the hymn is this: because God owns the cattle on a thousand hills, He will take care of us.

Because God owns the cattle, there will always be plenty of beef to go around. Since He is a good owner, He will always take care of those who need some beef! Amen!

God owns everything! The deed to the universe is in His name!

Think about this: You lay up treasure in heaven only as you lay down treasure on earth. The truth is: You don't own anything. God owns everything. Therefore, you can willingly surrender your desire for ownership with confidence, because you can trust the legitimate owner, God, to meet your every need.

# God Gives Man Power to Gain Wealth

It's a biblical fact. God owns everything. But He's not stingy. As a good God who loves His children and wants them to do good, He makes all He owns available to us, whom He has made in His likeness and image. (See Genesis 1:26-31.) Human beings are the only created creatures that are like the Creator. God is spirit, and He has given us a spirit. (See John 4:23-24.) God gave us the ability and opportunity to respond to Him spiritually. Only humans have the capacity to worship and reverence God. Our Creator made it possible for us to have a personal relationship with Him based on faith and obedience.

Our first ancestors, Adam and Eve, were put in a virtual paradise, the garden of Eden. God gave Adam and Eve authority and rule over all creation (v. 26). The Creator blessed them and charged them to be fruitful and multiply (v. 28). They were given the delightful assignment of prospering and bringing success to earth.

God's intention was for human beings to subdue the earth (to conquer and bring it under subjection, to bring it under control). Take charge. Be the boss. Supervise it. Manage its resources. God supplied plants and animals for food for the human race (vv. 29-30). When the Lord finished establishing Adam and Eve in the garden, He declared all that He had made and put in place to be "very good" (v. 31).

*Through the ages, we have subdued creation, taken authority over the earth, and caused it to prosper. In many ways, humankind has done well.*

Through the ages, we have subdued creation, taken authority over the earth, and caused it to prosper. In many ways, humankind has done well. We have been very successful in managing earth's vast material resources. We have created great wealth. Or have we?

In Deuteronomy chapter eight, Moses recites God's gracious dealings with the nation of Israel. He opens his inspiring sermon by reminding them of certain critical factors in their spiritual history. First, in verses 1-6, Moses charges the people to remember to be careful to do God's commandments. If they would, as their forefathers had, even though they were severely tested and humbled, they would prosper: live, multiply, and occupy the Promised Land promised to their fathers. Verse six sums this section up well.

*You shall keep the commandments of the Lord your God, to walk in His ways and to fear Him.*

Second, in verses 7-18 God speaks through Moses, charging and warning Israel to be careful when they enter the "good land" God is bringing them to. When they occupied this prosperous land of plenty, and had eaten their fair share of milk and honey, they were to bless the Lord for giving them the good land. Never forget to give credit where credit is due, Moses was saying. God made this prosperity possible for you.

While they were enjoying the bounties and abundant blessings of the Promised Land God had given them, Moses told them to beware. Be careful and beware. Beware of what? The human tendency to forget who made all of the prosperity, success, wealth, and good times possible in the first place.

When you have eaten and are satisfied and are enjoying the perks of the Promised Land, do not become proud in your heart and forget your God who is feeding and blessing you. Don't be tempted in your season of prosperity and success to say, "My power and the strength of my hand made me this wealth." (v. 17). Don't get fat and sassy, pointing your finger at yourself saying, look what I have done. That's grievously shortsighted, ungrateful nonsense. Israel didn't create their wealth. God did.

This is a vitally important stewardship principle. Not only does God own everything (as He did the Promised Land), He also gives people the power to prosper. God is the real power behind prosperity. Proverbs 10:22 declares that it is the blessing of the Lord that makes us rich. People don't make themselves rich. God does. Who owns the beef? God.

Moses didn't want God's chosen people to make a major lifestyle mistake, so he wisely and forthrightly exhorted them:

> *You shall remember the Lord your God, for it is He who is giving you power to make wealth, that He may confirm His covenant, which He swore to your forefathers, as it is to this day.*
> — Proverbs 10:18

The goodness of God, not the ingenuity of people, produces wealth. God brings gain to our lives. The power to prosper comes from God, not ourselves. Arrogance flies out the window when we remember that God is the source of our success. If wealth makes people proud, then those people understand neither themselves nor their wealth.

Not only does God own everything (as He did the Promised Land), He also gives people the power to prosper. God is the real power behind prosperity.

Humble, thankful people know where their wealth comes from. It comes from the hand of a good, gracious, and generous God.

Israel's prosperity in the Promised Land is proof of God's keeping the covenant (agreement) that He made in Genesis 12:1-3 with Abraham (to bless him and make him a blessing) and the spiritual fathers of the Jewish nation. According to Psalm 105:10, God's covenant is an "everlasting covenant." That sacred agreement between God and man remains in force today. It is a promise to all who are righteous and walk by faith and who are no longer under the curse of the Law.

> *Now that no one is justified by the Law before God is evident; for, "The righteous man shall live by faith." However, the Law is not of faith; on the contrary, "He who practices them shall live by them." Christ redeemed us from the curse of the Law, having become a curse for us — for it is written, "Cursed is everyone who hangs on a tree." In order that in Christ Jesus the blessing of Abraham might come to the Gentiles, so that we might receive the promise of the Spirit through faith.*
> — Galatians 3:11-14

This is freedom-producing revelation. Because we are redeemed from the curse of the Law through Christ, Abraham's promise of divine blessing is ours. As Christians, we stand in a long line of precious people of faith who have a promise from God for prosperity and success. That promise is fulfilled through a process of faithful stewardship.

This lesson is built on the three fundamental truths. First, God owns everything. Second, we manage His resources; He is the power behind our prosperity. Third, God alone is our source.

## God Is Man's Source for Everything

Recently in a tense counseling session, a deeply frustrated man defiantly told me, "Pastor, I don't need God. I don't need family or friends. I don't need you, anybody, or anything. I can run my life perfectly fine by myself. I don't depend upon anyone else but me."

Unfortunately, his bold declaration of independence and self-sufficiency was not working out in real life. His lovely wife and children, his employer, his

As Christians, we stand in a long line of precious people of faith who have a promise from God for prosperity and success. That promise is fulfilled through a process of faithful stewardship.

colleagues, and his extended family were all ready to give up on this guy. They were fed up with his independent spirit. He was a mess and he was messing up all of his relationships. His world was falling down all around him. Why? He thought he was self-sufficient. He had deluded himself into believing that dependence upon anything but himself was a sign of personal weakness. According to this anti-dependence crusader, he was his own source of supply for everything he thought he needed in life.

What a sad man! Arrogantly (and ignorantly I might add!), this disillusioned Lone Ranger boasted that he didn't look to anyone or anything else as his source for life. He alone was the center of his universe, the self-proclaimed king of his little kingdom that was bordered on the north, south, east, and west by I, me, mine, and myself.

People all wrapped up in themselves make a pretty small package!

I responded to his challenge by quoting what the Apostle wrote:

> *My God shall supply all your needs according to His riches in glory in Christ Jesus.*
> —Philippians 4:19

The apostle Paul was the John Wayne of the New Testament. This one-of-a-kind, Spirit-filled, gospel-slinging missionary to the Gentiles turned the world upside down and right side up (Acts 17:6). Spiritually, he was a man's man. Paul's academic training, his religious standing with the Sanhedrin before conversion, his leadership in the early church, his unparalleled eloquence, and his powerful, soul-penetrating, Holy Spirit-inspired pen set him far above the Christians of his day.

If anyone could have pointed to himself as a self-made man or rested on his moral and religious accomplishments, it certainly was Paul. He could have easily said, "Look at me. I have made myself what I am. I don't need anyone but myself to be successful."

He didn't! From the depth of Paul's humble heart and through the passionate words from his own mouth, we hear exactly the opposite. Unashamedly, Paul made it clear who his source in life was:

> *Such confidence we have through Christ toward God. Not that we are adequate in ourselves to consider anything as coming from ourselves, but*

If anyone could have pointed to himself as a self-made man or rested on his moral and religious accomplishments, it certainly was Paul. He could have easily said, "Look at me. I have made myself what I am. I don't need anyone but myself to be successful."

*our adequacy is from God, who made us adequate as servants of a new covenant, not of the letter, but of the Spirit; for the letter kills, but the Spirit gives life.*
— 2 Corinthians 3:4-6

*Not that I speak from want; for I have learned to be content in whatever circumstances I am. I know how to get along with humble means, and I also know how to live in prosperity; in any and every circumstance, I have learned the secret of being filled and going hungry, both of having abundance and suffering need. I can do all things through Him (Jesus Christ) who strengthens me.*
— Philippians 4:11-13

Paul's source was God. His adequacy in life and ministry came from the all-sufficient One. The great apostle had no doubt about it. His God, would, not might, meet his every need through the riches and glory of Jesus Christ. To Paul, what he wrote in Philippians 4:19 was a wonderful promise of divine provision that could be counted on. God, not Paul, would meet Paul's needs.

As a servant of the living God, Paul had learned how to depend upon the Lord to meet his every need. Whether circumstances were in his favor or not, whether material resources were abundant or lacking, Paul leaned on God, looking to Him to supply his needs.

One of God's names in the Old Testament is Jehovah-Jireh, which means "the Lord will provide" and "God's provision will be seen." The definition is found in Genesis 22:14 which reads, "Abraham called the name of that place 'The Lord will provide,' as it is said to this day, 'In the mount of the Lord I have provided.'"

Genesis 22 is the biblical setting for the revelation of God as provider. The chapter presents a moving story which focuses on the proving of Abraham's faith on Mount Moriah. God had asked Abraham to take his only son, Isaac, to Mount Moriah and sacrifice him there.

On the three-day journey to Mount Moriah, Isaac asked his father where the lamb was for the burnt offering (v. 7). Abraham answered, "God will provide for Himself the lamb for the burnt offering, my son. So the two of them walked on together" (v. 8). Imagine that was you and your only son. What would those three days have been like, knowing where you were going and what God had asked you to do? What would you have been thinking and feeling?

Abraham was full of faith. Upon their arrival at the place of sacrifice, Abraham

> One of God's names in the Old Testament is Jehovah-Jireh, which means "the Lord will provide" and "God's provision will be seen."

built the altar, arranged the wood, tied up his son, and laid him on top of the wood. Obeying God, Abraham raised the knife to slay his son. In response to Abraham's great faith, the Lord stopped the hand of Abraham from slaying Isaac. He commended Abraham's faith and love for God. Then He provided a ram in place of Isaac. The Lord provided. God's provision was evident.

Abraham trusted God to provide. So did Paul. Paul had learned that he could be content in every circumstance because God was His provider. His source. Paul was personally convinced that through Jesus Christ every need he would ever have would be met, and he could rise up and conquer every challenge through Christ's strength in him.

God not only owns the universe, He is the source of all creation. Lifestyle stewardship acknowledges God as our source. He alone is our source for everything. It's not us, our families, our relatives, the corporation we work for, Wall Street, the government, or any other persons or institutions that provide for our needs. God uses them as channels, but He is our ultimate source.

Stewardship, managing God's resources, is much simpler when we recognize God as our source.

> *The Lord is my shepherd, I shall not want…*
> — Psalm 23:1

*Lifestyle stewardship acknowledges God as our source. He alone is our source for everything. It's not us, our families, our relatives, the corporation we work for, Wall Street, the government, or any other persons or institutions that provide for our needs. God uses them as channels, but He is our ultimate source.*

# Five Follies of a Foolish Farmer

In Luke 12:16-21, Jesus introduces us to a man who didn't recognize God as his source. This story is told as an illustration of the principles taught in verses 13-15 where, as you remember, the Lord warned us to "be on guard against every form of greed."

In this parable of the rich man whose land had been very productive, five things standout as indictments against him because he mismanaged his resources. God ended up calling him a fool.

### 1. The Rich Man Forgot God (vv. 16-17)
This farmer's land had produced a bumper crop. He had personally prospered. But he failed to acknowledge where the abundant harvest and prosperity had come from! No mention of God at all. No stopping to give thanks to His Creator

for the bountiful harvest. No recognition of the Almighty whatsoever. Instead, after gloating over his overflow crop, he said, "What shall I do, since I have no place to store my crops?"

Notice that the personal pronouns "I" and "my" are used three times in one short sentence. "What shall I do?" not "God, what do You want me to do with the harvest?" And "my crops." But whose crops are they in reality? Where did the soil, seed, sunshine, water, growing climate, and workers to till the fields come from anyway? Who provided all the farmer needed to be so successful that his barns were too small to store the crop? Who was the true source of the farmer's blessing?

God blessed the farmer's life, but the farmer left God out of the plan. He should have stopped reasoning within himself, and turned his gaze heavenward to ask the Lord, "Sir, what would you have me to do with this abundance you have so graciously provided for me?"

He should have, could have; but he didn't. The foolish farmer forgot God.

## 2. He Became Greedy and Selfish (vs. 18)

This verse reveals the true state of this man's heart. In verses 17-19, he used some form of first person singular pronouns no less than eleven times! "I will," "my crops," "my barns," "my grain," "my good," "my ease." This guy was stuck on himself. Greed had its clutches in him. He was a completely selfish man. He had no thoughts for God or others.

His unilateral decision to build bigger barns was not wrong in itself. His reason for wanting them was wrong. He wanted larger storage places so he could keep every kernel of grain for himself. He thought he owned it, and he didn't believe he had to answer to anybody for it. This foolish farmer never saw beyond himself. He worshipped his grain-filled barns.

A school boy was once asked what parts of speech the words *my* and *mine* are. His answer? "Aggressive pronouns." The rich man in our parable was aggressively self-centered. He thought everything revolved around himself. Grain and greed became his gods.

> The Kingdom of Christ and of God will never belong to anyone who is impure or greedy, for a greedy person is really an idol worshipper. He loves and worships the good things of this life more than God.
> — Ephesians 5:5 TLB

The Kingdom of Christ and God will never belong to anyone who is impure or greedy — for a greedy person is really an idol worshipper. He loves and worships the good things of this life more than God.

## 3. He Forgot Other People  (v. 19)

Introverted, considering himself only, the farmer was elated to have so much that it would last for years. He was in fine shape because he had plenty of provision for the foreseeable future and beyond. No worry about lack for this self-centered farmer. He had it made — whether anybody else did or not.

Indeed, the farmer had more than enough for himself, but what about others? Were there any poor in his community? Any hungry people for whom his grain would provide a much needed blessing? What about his faithful workers? They might have liked to share in the bounty; after all they labored long and hard for him. Were there others whose crops hadn't come in as bountiful as his own? They might have had room in their barns for some of his grain.

The farmer couldn't find it in his heart to use some of his blessing to bless others less fortunate. He didn't have to give it all away. Just some. A portion would have been adequate. That's why God had blessed him.

But selfish people don't think about others. Sharing is not in their vocabulary. Greedy people want it all, and want to keep all of it. This blessed man could have torn down his barns to share the grain with others; instead, he build bigger barns, which became lifeless monuments to his selfish heart.

> Selfish people don't think about others. Sharing is not in their vocabulary. Greedy people want it all, and want to keep all of it.

That which could have become a blessing to others would soon become a curse to the self-centered farmer.

## 4. He Became Worldly and Lazy  (v. 19)

The farmer built bigger barns, relaxed, and threw a party. He lived a lavish, careless, carefree lifestyle. The rich man was, in actuality, very poor. "Eat, drink, and be merry" became his life's motto. He stopped contributing to life and became a consumer.

He patted himself on the back, congratulating himself for a job well done. His farm had produced a great crop. He had built new storage facilities that could be seen for miles around. Everyone knew that he was extremely wealthy. He lived the lifestyle of a rich and famous person, flaunting his wealth for all the world to see. Unconcerned for others,  unrestrained in his preoccupation with himself, he was unwilling to share.

Greed and selfishness turn our attention inward. The temptation to stop working, to become worldly, to gratify our fleshly desires, and to ignore the needs of our fellow human beings, becomes more easy with each passing day.

The foolish farmer needed a wake-up call.

One came.

## 5. The Foolish Farmer Lost it All  (vv. 20-21)

The day of reckoning arrived. While the farmer was partying, God spoke to him. "Hey you! You fool! Tonight you are going to die, and you can't take your wealth with you. When you're gone, who is going to own what you have prepared?"

You thought it was yours. It really isn't.

Jesus said death was coming and the rich man's stuff was staying behind. What was he going to do? He would be standing before his Maker very soon. What kind of account would he give of his stewardship of the resources God had blessed him with? How would he justify his lifestyle, in light of God's Word? What about all the good he could have done with his prosperity?

Men can forget God; but God always has the last word! The foolish farmer lost all he had because he focused on what doesn't last. His folly? He failed to realize that not only his possessions, but also his soul belonged to God. He was investing in the wrong place. He had denied God's rightful place in his overall life. He had willfully rejected a steward's lifestyle. God owned everything, the farmer included, and now it was time to square up accounts.

God promises to meet our need, not our greed. The verdict is expressed in verse 21. "So is the man who lays up treasure for himself, and is not rich toward God."

The formula for foolishness: Live for yourself, not for God. Store up treasure for yourself, not God and others.

God labeled the farmer a fool because the farmer had failed to be a good steward. He had chosen not to acknowledge God as owner of everything, and as His source, He had chosen not to manage his God-given resources in a faithful manner.

In the light of Luke 12:21, are you rich in things, or rich toward the Savior?

God promises to meet our need, not our greed.

# Everything That Is, Is His

## OWNERSHIP EXERCISE

Thoroughly read and study David's prayer in 1 Chronicles, then respond to the exercise that follows.

*David blessed the Lord in the sight of all the assembly; and David said, "Blessed art Thou, O Lord God of Israel our father forever and ever. Thine, O Lord, is the greatness and the power and the glory and the victory and the majesty, indeed everything that is in the heavens and the earth; Thine is the dominion, O Lord, and Thou dost exalt Thyself as head over all. Both riches and honor come from Thee, and Thou dost rule over all, and in Thy hand is power and might; and it lies in Thy hand to make great, and to strengthen everyone. Now therefore, our God, we thank Thee, and praise Thy glorious name. But who am I and who are my people, that we should be able to offer as generously as this? For all things come from Thee, and from Thy hand we have given Thee. For we are sojourners before Thee, and tenants, as all our fathers were; our days on the earth are like a shadow, and there is no hope. O Lord our God, all this abundance that we have provided to build Thee a house for Thy holy name, it is from Thy hand, and all is Thine.*
— 1 Chronicles 29:10-16

1. Make a list of all the adjectives David uses to describe God.

   _____

   _____

2. List His attributes (dominion).

   _____

   _____

   _____

3. Where does David say riches, honor, and abundance come from?

   _____

4. David said we are tenants on earth. What is a tenant? What do they do?

   _____

5. Who gave the people the ability to give a generous offering for the construction of the Temple?

   _____

6. Who gives you the ability to give?

   _____

   _____

7. David declared "all things come from Thee." Do you agree? List at least ten major things in your life that have come from God.

   _____

   _____

   _____

   _____

8. Study Matthew 7:9-11, Job 38:41, and Matthew 6:25-34. In your own words write about God being the great provider for His children.

   _____

   _____

## Something to Think About

Your employer downsizes and you are laid off your job. No more paycheck. The national economy goes belly up and the stock market crashes. You lose your savings and investments. The government collapses and cannot provide humanitarian services for society. Where will you turn? Who will be your source for what you need?

> God is your source because He owns the cattle on a thousand hills!

Decide now that in all situations, no matter what, God and God alone is your source. If everything else falls, He stands. God's Kingdom will never downsize. Heaven's bank will never declare bankruptcy. Kingdom stock will only increase. No one will ever knock Jesus Christ off the throne! God is an inexhaustible, unlimited source. His kingdom is stable, secure, and more than able to meet your every need.

God is your source because He owns the cattle on a thousand hills!

## Confession of Faith

I acknowledge that God is the owner of all things.
He is my Maker and Redeemer. I am accountable to Him for my life
and the lifestyle I choose to live.
I trust God as my source.
I will give Him the glory for prospering me.
By faith, I will honor, respect, and obey His stewardship principles.
As He blesses me, I will bless others in His name.

# Lesson 3

## Stewardship 102: We Manage the Ranch

*Let a man regard us in this manner, as servants of Christ, and stewards of the mysteries of God. In this case, moreover, it is required of stewards that one be found trustworthy.*
— 1 Corinthians 4:1-2

### PRINCIPLE

• Man manages what God owns.

### PURPOSE

The purpose of this lesson is to demonstrate that man has been appointed as a manager, or caretaker, of all that God owns. Stewards are guardians who watch over, give oversight to, and care for the resources the Lord has entrusted to them. Man is given authority to manage and is accountable to God for that management. Managers are to be found faithful, or trustworthy, in carrying out their duties.

### DISCUSSION

"Under New Management." The brightly colored banner was strung across the entrance to a highly visible restaurant. It had opened a year earlier with much hype and fanfare. Initially, it was very popular. The parking lots were always jammed. Diners raved about the excellent cuisine. Prices were reasonable. But the restaurant had an Achilles heel. The service was lousy. Waiters and waitresses didn't seem to care if you were there. It took forever to be seated, and another forever to get served. The restaurant closed its doors within twelve months.

It opened with a big bang, and closed with a whimper and a sigh. The reason? Poor management.

These owners wanted to succeed. But the management team failed miserably. They did not take their responsibility seriously. Their job was to represent the owners' interests by providing customers with an outstanding dining experience. If they succeeded as caretakers, dinner guests would return, positive word would spread throughout the community, and the business would flourish.

Man is given authority to manage and is accountable to God for that management. Managers are to be found faithful, or trustworthy, in carrying out their duties.

By successfully serving people, they would have undoubtedly shown a profit. The owners would have been happy and, hopefully, passed on the rewards of success to the management team and their staff. But the managers missed the mark. They were found untrustworthy, unfaithful in their assignment.

New owners with a new management team took over. They remodeled the exterior and hired new staff. They provided a money-back guarantee if service was not exceptional. They went to all of this effort and expense to try and overcome the previous restaurant's reputation for poor service and poor management.

# Christians Are Under New Management

When a person comes to Christ and is born again (John 3:3), they become a new creature. For new Christians, one of the most cherished verses in the Bible is found in 2 Corinthians 5:17. Here Paul explains the results of the new birth.

> *If any man is in Christ, he is a new creature; the old things passed away; behold, new things have come.*

Life isn't the same after we are saved. Praise God! We become new creatures (persons) through our relationship with Jesus. We look pretty much the same on the outside, but we are brand new on the inside! Our old man, with it's self-centered lifestyle and old ways of doing things, is passed away.

A miraculous change has come about. Everything about us becomes new! We are new people with a new beginning, spiritually renewed and recreated in the image of Christ. Our old man is gone and buried. A new man is born and raised to life in Christ Jesus. (See Ephesians 4:22-24 and Colossians 3:6-14.)

No longer dominated by Satan and self, we surrender by faith, the rights of our life to the lordship of Jesus Christ. We die to self, and live to Him. (See Galatians 2:20 and Romans 6:1-13). We choose to live for God, not ourselves. We come under new management — God's management. Because He bought us with the precious price of the blood of His Son, we belong to Him (1 Corinthians 6:19-20). We grant God lordship, headship, and leadership over our lives.

Life isn't the same after we are saved. Praise God! We become new creatures (persons) through our relationship with Jesus. We look pretty much the same on the outside, but we are brand new on the inside!

# Christians Manage God's Ranch

Along with our new relationship and new life in Christ comes a new role. In 1 Corinthians 4:1-2, Paul gives the purpose of the Christian life:

*Let a man regard us in this manner, as servants of Christ, and stewards of the mysteries of God. In this case, moreover, it is required of stewards that one be found trustworthy.*

Men and women of the world take notice. We Christians are, first, servants of Christ, and second, stewards of God. Following the example of our Master, we are on this earth to serve. We are servants for Christ's sake. We choose a lifestyle of service.

Our service is expressed through our stewardship. Biblically, a steward can be defined as "the manager of a household or estate." Dictionaries define a steward as one who actively directs the affairs of others — a manager. Synonyms for stewards are "caretakers," "guardians," and "overseers."

A steward is a manager, a person entrusted with managing something that belongs to another. Owners of homes, estates, businesses, corporations, ministries, and public and private services all need managers, people specifically assigned to oversee the operation of the business. God owns a Kingdom. He reigns over it supremely as King. Successful operation of the Kingdom of God requires faithful managers to carry out its holy purposes.

A steward is a manager, a person entrusted with managing something that belongs to another.

First Chronicles 28:1 illustrates from Scripture the concept of stewards as overseers of another's property:

*David assembled at Jerusalem all the officials of Israel, the princes of the tribes, and the commanders of the divisions that served the king, and the commanders of thousands, and the commanders of hundreds, and the overseers of all the property and livestock belonging to the king and his sons, with the officials and the mighty men, even the valiant men.*

Overseers managed the property and livestock of King David and his sons. As king, David owned the cattle while appointed overseers (stewards) managed the beef!

Christian stewards manage the Gospel work of God's Kingdom on this earth. Those who name the name of Christ represent the King and His interests. In the last chapter, we learned that God owns everything. He owns the cattle. Someone has to manage the ranch where those cattle are. That's us. His stewards — managers of His beef!

Christian stewards manage the Gospel work of God's Kingdom on this earth. Those who name the name of Christ represent the King and His interests.

## PERSONAL REFLECTION

1.  Describe in your own words what you believe a manager is.

    _____
    _____
    _____

2.  Have you ever been in the position of "manager" over something? What did you manage and how did you manage it?

    _____
    _____

3.  What are the joys of managing? The pressures? The rewards?

    _____
    _____
    _____

4.  What do you see as the minimum requirements needed for a person to be a successful manager?

    _____
    _____
    _____

5.  What do you believe you, as a Christian, are called to manage?

    _____
    _____
    _____

# Survival, Success, or Significance?

There are three major ways to look at life. People generally fit into one of these categories.

## 1. Survival

By far, the majority of people on planet Earth are suvivors. Survival is the name of their game. Their rules are few and simple. A survivor's vision is small, very limited. They have tunnel vision, living in a world bordered by I, me, mine, and myself. They live for the present, regret the past, fear the future. They are "now" people, supreme consumers who live for the moment.

The survivor's focus is self-centered. "Their agenda" is all that matters. Their goal in life is simply to survive, hold on, hang in there, hope it works out. They are "get by" people, committed to minimum living — What is the least I have to do to make it? — They are takers, not givers. Survivors have no concept of service or stewardship. They see life as hard, without reward, and something you just have to survive. They have no dreams of success, and certainly no thoughts of significance.

Survivors are a sorry lot, who get in the way of God's great plan for mankind. Bible Examples: Jacob, Aaron, Joseph's brothers, Judas, the unfaithful steward.

## 2. Success

These folks choose to move from the ranks of survivor to success. They speak and seek success. They are committed to being successful, making it in life. They want to be on top. Winning is everything. Their vision is a little broader than a survivor, a larger world, that does include others. But it's mostly others who can help them succeed in accomplishing their goals and fulfilling their dreams!

Success-oriented people focus on their own and other people's agendas. Family, friends, and business associates are important in their world. "Our agenda" takes center stage. Success means helping those they love. After that they will help others. Success-oriented people focus on the future. They work hard in the present. They choose to forget the past.

The allure of "success" and becoming successful in the world's eyes is what drives these people to get ahead. They loathe the survivor's "get by" attutude. They want to forge ahead; climb new mountains; conquer challenges. Their goal is to move forward in life, ahead of others, and look good in the process. They are still more often than not largely consumers, but they do give more than survivors. Their giving is geared to making them successful.

Success, at any cost, is the goal of purely success-oriented people. Bible examples: Rich young ruler, Gehazi, prodigal son, Ahab and Jezebel.

## 3. Significance

Few people attain this level of living. Significance-minded people soar above the crowd. They are frustrated by survivors, and envied by the successful. Their

> The survivor's focus is self-centered. Their "agenda" is all that matters. Their goal in life is simply to survive, hold on, hang in there, hope it works out.

> Success-oriented people focus on their own and other people's agendas. Family, friends, and business associates are important in their world.

vision is of a wide, wide world. They are big thinkers who live for time and eternity. They care about eternal things, values and issues that really matter. Influence. Making a difference in life is their agenda. "Also-ran" is not in their vocabulary. Winning is important, but not everything; it's the way you play and the way you win.

Their focus is "this one thing I do." God's kingdom and His agenda are important to them. They care about every precious person and how to impact them for Christ. They are contributors, not consumers. They live to give. They're willing to sacrifice in order to serve.

Maximum energy and effort is their modus operandi. "Give it your all" is their motto. They live to be blessed so they can be a blessing to others. They strive to make a name for God in this life. They want to leave a legacy, a lasting impression and influence on mankind for God's eternal Kingdom.

Significant people make a mark on humanity that is not soon forgotten. Bible examples: Jesus, Paul, Moses, Esther, Peter, heroes of faith in Hebrews 11.

## Stewards Are Significant People!

Survival, success, or significance. Which one means "servants of Christ, and stewards of the mysteries of God" (1 Corinthians 4:1)? Significance, of course! A biblical steward's vision is worldwide and Kingdom sized. They are huge-thinking, big-believing people. God's managers stay focused on the glory of God and the temporal and eternal good of mankind. Christian stewards are contributors. They are extraordinarily generous givers of time, talent, and treasure. Their lifestyle inspires other people to do better. It motivates people to strive for the Lord's very best in everything. They influence others to trust the Lord to meet their needs. Stewards assist others, by word and deed, in accomplishing God's great plan for prosperity and success in their lives.

Stewards are significant people. They make a significant difference in the lives of others because Jesus has made a significant difference in their lives. They joyfully and faithfully share what they have found: an abundant and properous life in Christ.

Stewardship is accepting from God personal responsiblity for all of life and the lifestyle we choose to live. Successful stewards can influence others positively and can powerfully impact their lives for time and eternity.

Significant people make a mark.

Servanthood plus stewardship equals significance. If you want to make a difference in people's lives, and I trust you do, then serve them, and bless them as you faithfully manage God's resources entrusted to you.

Managing God's resources is a high, holy, and significant calling.

## Stewards Are Faithful People

Everything we have is from God. We are simply holding it in trust. Therefore, it is our solemn duty to use it for Him. Take careful note of the sole scriptural requirement Paul makes of stewards of the gospel: "It is required of stewards that one be found trustworthy."

It is required — mandatory. Not optional. No take it or leave it here. Stewards must be trustworthy. They must be found worthy of trust, observed by God and others, day in and day out, doing what God has commanded them to do. They must be faithful in carrying out their assigned tasks. Full of faith. Motivated by faith, and marked by trust. Stewards must be managers who believe in God, His kingdom, and who are themselves believable. Trusted by God and men.

If you are a faithful steward, then:

- You are a person of impeccable personal integrity. You are who you say you are, and you do what you say you will do.
- You can be counted on because you count it a privilege and joy to be counted worthy of a management job in the Kingdom.
- You are believable because you believe in God, His mission, and your role as a Christian witness and ambassador for Christ in this world.
- You can be trusted with whatever God sends you to do because you trust His Word and you trust yourself to obey it.
- You can stand confidently before the Lord with a clear conscience knowing that you fulfilled God's special assignment for you.

Faithfulness must be evident in the lifestyle of God's stewards. Successful managers of God's resources are people who live a lifestyle of faith.

## Five Features of a Faithful Steward

In the last chapter we examined the story in Luke 12:16-21 about a foolish farmer who proved to be an unfaithful steward. Luke 19:11-26 presents another

Stewardship is accepting from God personal responsiblity for all of life and the lifestyle we choose to live. Successful stewards can influence others positively and can powerfully impact their lives for time and eternity.

parable about stewardship. The key figure in this story is a slave who proved faithful to his master.

Near Jerusalem, Jesus gave a teaching on stewardship as a picture of the spiritual principles that govern God's Kingdom. The crowd that followed the Lord thought that the kingdom would appear immediately. In response to their anticipation, as well as misjudgment in timing, the Master told them the following story about a certain nobleman who went away to receive a kingdom.

A nobleman, who was already a wealthy landowner, was summoned to a foreign country where he was to inherit, or receive, a kingdom. More land. But he would not settle there. He had every intention of returning, and he gave his slaves/servants specific instructions about what they were to do in his absence. He called ten of his slaves, and gave them ten minas, and said to them, "Do business with this until I come." (vv. 12-13)

These ten slaves were told to manage his business. Each slave was given the equivalent of 100 days wages, ($20.00 in today's currency.) The slaves were then dismissed to conduct profitable business for their master.

Not all of the people under the nobleman's leadership liked him. Verse 14 tells us that a delegation of disgruntled citizens followed the nobleman to the foreign country, with the sole purpose of tarnishing his reputation in the new kingdom he was to receive. They wanted to make him look bad.

Despite organized opposition, the nobleman prevailed, received the new kingdom, and returned home. He ordered the ten slaves to come before him and give him an account of their business dealings (v. 15).

The first slave appeared before the nobleman and reported, "Master, your mina has made ten minas more" (v. 16). A ten-fold increase. One thousand percent gain! Not bad at all. The slave had gone to work and faithfully conducted business. The money made money. Twenty dollars became two hundred dollars. The nobleman was feeling pretty good about the slave's increase. Verse 17 tells us he said to the slave, "Well done, good slave, because you have been faithful in a very little thing, be in authority over ten cities."

Well done, my man! Great job! You are a good slave. You have been faithful with my twenty dollars. So faithful, that you handed me back two hundred. Such a small amount has become a large amount. Why? You, my good slave, have been faithful in a very little thing. I am pleased. I couldn't be happier with

Successful managers of God's resources are people who live a lifestyle of faith.

your business performance. What a tremendous report. I am so thrilled about your success that I am putting you in charge over ten cities. As of this moment, you are promoted from slave to supervisor. No longer will you take orders. You will give them.

He had been faithful in a small thing, and he was promoted to a big thing! Faithfulness was the key to his reward.

A second slave also reported a gain. He was also rewarded according to his faithfulness (vv. 18-19). But in verses 19-27, we read of another slave, one who proved unfaithful in the discharge of his business duties. Instead of rewards, he was embarassed, humiliated, and punished (v. 24). It was not a good day for the slave who chose to be an unfaithful manager.

Five characteristics distinguish the "good slave" from the bad slave who failed to prosper his master.

## 1. The Good Slave Recognized and Respected His Master

The nobleman was the boss, the person in charge. The slave submitted himself to his lawful and rightful master. Nowhere in this dialogue does the slave refer to himself. No personal pronouns. Just a quiet, but powerful acknowedgment of the master's position, power, and right to ask and expect his slave to do business for him.

The good slave trusted the nobleman and showed him respect. He did his best to please his master with a positive return on the master's money.

*Do you respect God as your Lord and Master?*

## 2. The Good Slave Did Business for the Master

The good slave obeyed the instructions of the nobleman with no questions. He didn't hesitate. He was loyal to his master. He was told what to do, so he set out to do it. No doubting, no undermining authority, no second guessing. He simply went to work. Knowing the master expected a return, the good slave labored in such a way as to guarantee a return.

*Are you conducting your Master's business?*

## 3. The Good Slave Forgot About Himself

In contrast, the slave who was afraid of his master worried for himself, while the faithful slave went to work for his boss. This business deal was all about the master and his money, not the slave and his concerns. The faithful slave was fully focused on the task at hand: Do business for the master.

No emotional distractions. Nothing deterred him from accomplishing the goal. The good slave set aside his personal agenda for the time being, and set out to do the nobleman's agenda. He invested the nobleman's money and presented him with a huge return when he returned from his journey.

*Do you do God's business for yourself, or for Him?*

## 4. The Good Slave Was Blessed by His Master

We have discussed the generous reward he received. The amount of the reward must have been beyond the slave's wildest imagination. His master was obviously a very generous sort who put a high premium on faithfulness. Faithfulness was a top priority to this nobleman. The good slave rose to a position of prominence and prosperity, because he too, valued faithfulness.

*Do you expect God to bless you for being a faithful manager?*

## 5. The Good Slave Received Even More Reward

When life is good, it's really good! When the money was taken away from the unfaithful slave, guess who it was given to? The good slave who was given authority over ten cities. Why did the ten mina guy get another mina? Because he could be trusted with it.

Jesus said in verse 26, "I tell you, that to everyone who has shall more be given." Faithful, trustworthy stewards can expect to be blessed again, and again, and again! That's the way it is in the Kingdom of God.

*Can you think of a time when God overwhelmingly blessed you because of your faithful stewardship? How did it feel to receive more than expected?*

## SUMMARY

Opportunities for stewardship will come. Participation is a choice. Faithful stewardship doesn't come naturally. It demands work and effort. We will eventually give account for our management. Faithful stewardship will be rewarded handsomely.

> Opportunities for stewardship will come. Participation is a choice.
>
> Faithful stewardship doesn't come naturally. It demands work and effort.
>
> We will eventually give account for our management. Faithful stewardship will be rewarded handsomely.

# Stewardship Is a Partnership

This lesson has been entitled Stewardship 102: He owns the cattle, we manage the ranch. Owning cattle and managing a ranch require a partnership. A faithful God (the owner) and faithful children of God (the managers) can form a fruitful, mutually satisfying partnership.

The stewardship process is a partnership, a divine/human arrangement. He does His part, we do our part — God and man working together to accomplish God's will on earth.

The stewardship process is a partnership, a divine/human arrangement.

Mark 4:26-27 contains the Parable of the Seed. This kingdom parable is a perfect illustration of the divine/human partnership process.

> *The Kingdom of God is like a man who casts seed upon the soil; and goes to bed at night and gets up by day, and the seed sprouts up and grows — how, he himself does not know. The soil produces crops by itself; first the blade, then the head, then the mature grain in the head. But when the crop permits, he immediately puts in the sickle, because the harvest has come.*

Seed. Soil. Harvest. This is a parable about a process where small seeds turn into a huge harvest. How? Through a partnership. God does His part. Man does his part.

## Man's Part I: Sow the Seed (vv. 26-27)
The farmer in the parable does what farmers do — sows seed. The seed sprouts and grows. How — he doesn't know and he probably doesn't care. But he does know that it has grown. Something happened to that seed once it went in the soil. The seed is now a plant. He weeds and feeds the field as farmers do. Then, when the time comes, he will harvest what he has sown.

God does His part. Man does his part....God doesn't sow seed. That's the farmer's job. But God certainly can grow it.

## God's Part I: Grow the Seed! (v. 28)
God did what God does. He created the seed and soil to work together to produce growth. Soil produces crops. It's an orderly, purposeful process built in nature by the Creator — seed, blade, head, mature grain. God doesn't sow seed. That's the farmer's job. But God certainly can grow it. The farmer can't come close to doing that on his own.

### Man's Part II: Mow the Seed! (v. 29)

The farmer sowed the seed. God grew it. Now the farmer will take the sickle while the harvest is ripe and harvest it. Get it in the barns and to market. God and farmer bringing in a harvest together. He'll keep some seed from the grain for the next crop. Seed to seed. The process is complete.

## PARTNERSHIP PRINCIPLES

We sow the seed, God grows the seed. We can't grow the seed. God won't sow the seed. We mow the seed, only after we sow the seed and God grows the seed! We know we will mow the seed if we sow the seed because God will grow the seed.

### Management Inventory

Lifestyle stewardship is the faithful management of God's resources on a daily basis. Managers who are faithful and prosperous recognize and respect the partnership of the stewardship process. God does His part, we do our part. We can't do His part. He won't do our part. Take a look at your part through the following inventory exercise.

1. Get alone with God and open your eyes to His many gifts in your life.
2. Make a list of all He has given you.
3. Give thanks for each item on the list.
4. Honestly answer the hard question "How am I managing God's gifts?"
5. How would you describe your management style?
6. What kind of manager would your best friends say you are?
7. How can you be more faithful as a steward of God's resources?
8. Here's your action plan for improving your management style immediately.
   I will _____
   I plan _____
   I will share my plan with _____

## REMEMBER

He owns the cattle; we manage the ranch!

> We sow the seed, God grows the seed. We can't grow the seed. God won't sow the seed. We mow the seed, only after we sow the seed and God grows the seed!

# Lesson 4

## Attitudes of a Successful Steward

*Whether then you eat or drink or whatever you do, do all to the glory of God. Give no offense either to Jews or to Greeks or to the church of God; just as I also please all men in all things, not seeking my own profit, but the profit of many, that they may be saved.*
— 1 Corinthians 10: 31-33

### PRINCIPLE

- Your attitude is more important than your ability.

### PURPOSE

Years ago, the Stanford Research Institute released these findings regarding reasons for success in life: Ability 12%. Attitude 83%. Other 5%.

Success depends more upon attitude than ability. We will see from Scripture that successful stewards have adopted and acted upon a certain set of attitudes that unsuccessful stewards haven't. These particular attitudes distinguish faithful managers from unfaithful managers. They show who has strength, courage, and loyalty when it comes to managing God's resources successfully. These attitudes must be present if a person is to meet the requirement of being a trustworthy steward.

Success depends more upon attitude than ability.

### DISCUSSION

Stewardship means utilizing God-given abilities to manage God-given resources to accomplish God-ordained goals. In order to accomplish this we must maintain a certain set of attitudes. We must acknowledge that attitudes underlie our actions. Attitudes set the direction for the course we choose to take in life.

Attitudes shape the steward's philosophy and practices. It is imperative that God's stewards have the right attitudes if they are to soar above mediocrity to reap the highest and best rewards the Lord gives to faithful managers of His resources.

Our attitudes make or break us. Stewardship begins with our attitude.

# Attitude Adjustments

When I came to Christ at twenty years of age, Jesus changed my life. He created a "new heart" and put "a new spirit" within me (Ezekiel 36:26-28, 1 Peter 1:22-23). But I still retained my old, worldly thought life. My mind (thinking and attitudes) needed to be renewed. As I studied the Word and submitted myself to its transforming power (Romans 12:1-2), I realized that I needed some major attitude adjustments.

Philippians 2:5-15 is a commentary on Jesus Christ's attitude. Verse 5 commands Christians to have this attitude in themselves which was also in Christ Jesus. Our Savior's attitude is our perfect example to follow. We are to imitate His attitude toward life. The overall attitude that governed the Lord's earthly life and defined His daily lifestyle was marked by humility, an unselfish spirit, servanthood, and obedience to God's will. Jesus emptied Himself (v. 7) and humbled Himself to the point of dying on a cross for sinners (v. 8). God's Son obeyed His Father. His substitute death was not in vain. Christ's attitude and subsequent action led to salvation for humanity.

God honored and rewarded the self-sacrificing, servant's attitude of Jesus by exalting His name above every other name. He is Lord. Men bow before Him, because He died for them.

Paul specifically addresses believers who confess Jesus as Lord. In verses 12-15, the Apostle of grace exhorts us that with fear and trembling (which means to be sober minded and very serious about what God has done for you) we are to work out our salvation. In other words, our actions are to exemplify what God has worked in us. Our outward life is to manifest the new, inner life given to us. Working out our salvation covers many areas. But one area we must tackle for certain is this: changing our attitudes.

The Apostle tells us, in verse 14, to do all things without grumbling or disputing. No griping and fighting. We are to avoid a bad disposition and attitude. Why? We want to prove ourselves to be God's children. We must live blameless, innocent lives that are above reproach, if we are to shine as lights before a crooked and perverse generation.

The bottom line for Paul was this: Serve this world in the Savior's name. If this spiritually dark, lost, and dying world is ever to come to Christ, we must show them Christ's attitude.

Serve this world in the Savior's name. If this spiritually dark, lost, and dying world is ever to come to Christ, we must show them Christ's attitude.

Someone once said that the trouble with being a good sport is that you have to lose to prove it. Painfully true, isn't it? Jesus taught that we must lose our life to find it (Matthew 10:38-39).

To find Christ-like attitudes, I had to lose the worldly attitudes that had been shaped by my background and upbringing. The makeover of my mind proved to be quite a process. My two-decade-old attitudes were well entrenched.

The story is told of a positive thinking Cajun woman who lived in a small house in the Louisiana bayou country. She loved it. However, she was surrounded by negative-thinking neighbor ladies who grumbled and complained about "living way out here in the lonely, desolate, back country."

One day the woman had heard enough. "You live on the bayou. The bayou connects to the river. The river flows to the gulf. The gulf flows to the ocean. And the ocean touches the shores of the countries of the world. You all have boats. You can go anywhere from where you are!"

So can we! I needed an attitude adjustment. More like an overhaul! To be right and live right, we must think right. I am so thankful that God is patient, looooong-suffering and understanding. He knew I wasn't where I needed to be. My heavenly Father also knew where He could lead me. His grace being sufficient for a worldly-minded person like me meant I could start where I was and go to where I wanted to be. God's like that. He meets us where right we are and takes us to where we need to be. Hallelujah!

If it was to be, it was up to me. I could adjust my thinking if I really wanted to. You can do the same.

I believe it was William James who said, "You are where you are and what you are because of the dominating thoughts that occupy your mind." My most dominant thoughts and attitudes were self-centered. A poverty lifestyle had hardened my heart. Rebelling against the pain of doing without, I decided that the world existed for me, not me for it. Everything the earth had to give was mine for the taking. People were to be used. They were there to serve me, not for me to serve them.

Life, as I saw it, was all about me and what I wanted.

I had no idea what stewardship was. Solid, well-balanced, biblical teaching and Christ-like role models were foreign to my growing-up experience. No one

> To find Christ-like attitudes, I had to lose the worldly attitudes that had been shaped by my background and upbringing.

ever told me that God owns the cattle, and we manage the ranch. Personal fame, fortune, riches, power, and influence were the name of the game for me. My all-consuming, controlling attitude was "move over world, here I come." I planned to take from everyone all that I could so that I could prove I was somebody.

This new Christian was a long way away from emptying, humbling, and sacrificing himself. I had a lot to learn about being like Jesus in thought, word and deed. I had never been taught that attitudes are nothing more than habits of thought — and that habits can be acquired.

## REFLECTION

Have you ever thought the way I did? Think about your attitudes. What has shaped them? If you have changed your attitudes, how did you escape the old ones?

## POINT FOR PRAISE

If you have been delivered from poor attitudes, stop right now and give thanks to God. Praise Him for setting you free from what Zig Ziglar calls "stinking thinking."

Just a thought! We cannot direct the wind, but we can adjust our sails!

# Christlike Attitude in Action: Luke 10: 25-37

Our attitude tells the world what we expect from life. Faithful stewards have "Attitude" with a capital A. They expect to succeed.

Our attitude tells the world what we expect from life. Faithful stewards have "Attitude" with a capital A. They expect to succeed.

The parable of the Good Samaritan is not just a story of God's great love. It's also an outstanding example of Christ-like attitude in action — an attitude of self-sacrificing love expressed through faithful management of God's resources.

This teaching came in direct response to a lawyer who stood up and questioned Jesus concerning the Law of God. In verse 25, Scripture tells us that the attorney asked Jesus, "Teacher, what shall I do to inherit eternal life?" On the surface, this seems like a sincere inquiry. It wasn't. The lawyer was putting Jesus to the test, trying to trap the Master, trip Him up.

Recognizing the trap, Jesus answered the lawyer's question with one of his own. "What is written in the Law?" How does it read to you? (v. 26). The lawyer replied quoting Deuteronomy 6:5, which says the law is summed up in loving God and loving your neighbor as yourself.

Jesus responded, "You have answered correctly; do this, and you will live" (v. 28). If you will go out and love God and people, you will have the eternal life you asked about.

The lawyer knew this, but he didn't want to do it. Verse 29 reveals the lawyer's true attitude. He said to Jesus, "And who is my neighbor?" The implication here was that if he didn't know who his neighbor was then he didn't have to love them.

Jesus replied to the lawyer's attempt at self-justification with a story about neighbors. A man on his way to Jericho was robbed, brutally beaten, and left for dead.

Three types of men with very differing attitudes participated in this emergency.

## Attitude Number One (v. 30)
What is yours is mine and I'm going to take it!

This attitude is represented by the robbers. Sadistic, selfish, and incredibly uncaring men, their purpose was to take what belonged to others. They would do whatever it took to steal from someone. In this case, it meant nearly beating a man to death, stripping him naked, and leaving him on a desolate roadside to die.

What's yours is mine. It doesn't rightfully belong to me, but soon it will be mine anyway. I will take it by force if I have to.

The robbers didn't trust God or anybody else to take care of them. Their philosophy: I take care of myself by taking your things from you.

An innocent man was robbed, thrown in a ditch to die, wondering why in the world this had happened to him. He was victimized by people who saw him not as a neighbor, but as a target.

To those men, stewardship was a curse, certainly not a blessing. Their attitude was: God-given resources are to be stolen.

## Attitude Number Two (vv. 31-32)
What is mine is mine and I'm going to keep it!

Two religious men, a Priest and a Levite, both saw the victimized traveler. Both decided not to get involved. They even crossed to the other side of the road to avoid him. Maybe they were on their way to the Temple, some religious duty or observance to perform. This was inconvenient. It would make them unclean. They didn't want to get involved, thought they didn't have time to assist this dying man. — My time is my time. My money is my money. My reputation is mine.

Their response to this golden opportunity to help a helpless, hurting human being was "Thanks but no thanks. You're no neighbor to be assisted. You are a nuisance to be avoided." They were so self-involved that they didn't have time to help anyone.

Their attitude was: "Don't bother me and I won't bother you. You are on your own, buster."

These men of the cloth and the Book were accountable for the opportunity, and accountable for sharing their time and resources with the disabled man, but they didn't lift a finger. They looked the other way, hoping that passing by would somehow make them no longer responsible.

They preached the law of love in the Temple, but broke the law of love on the street.

This attitude is one of legalism. It says rules supersede relationships. "Don't break the rules, even if a defenseless man is dying in the ditch." Bound by suffocating doctrine, these religious hypocrites proved to be unfit of the title of faithful stewards.

Their attitude toward stewardship: God-given resources are to be accumulated and hoarded.

## Attitude Number Three (vv. 33-35)

What is mine is yours and I'm going to give it.

Finally, a Samaritan came upon the dying man, saw his life-threatening dilemma, and felt compassion. This man did not pass by. He jumped in the ditch to help. His heart hurt for the victim. He reached out.

He tore some of his clothes, improvising bandages. Next he generously poured oil and wine on the open wounds. Gently, he settled him on a beast (probably the Samaritan's own donkey) and transported him to a roadside inn. He told the innkeeper to shelter the man from robbers, the elements, and religious hypocrites. He asked the innkeeper to provide the man with clothes, a warm bed, nourishing food, medicine, and whatever else he might need.

The Samaritan said to spend however much money it took to care for the injured man, to nurse him back to health, and when he returned in a few days, he would reimburse all the expenses.

This man's attitude toward stewardship: God-given resources are to be valued, managed well, and shared.

The Good Samaritan, a man probably used to being shunned himself because of his ethnicity, was a faithful steward. He unhesitatingly shared what God had given him with a man who desperately needed what God could give through him. He risked his own life and expended his personal resources. Why? The love of God was in his heart.

After telling the story, Jesus asked the lawyer, "Which of these three do you think proved to be a neighbor to the man who fell into the robber's hands?" The answer is obvious. The lawyer responded, "The one who showed mercy toward him" (v. 37).

In effect, he was telling everyone listening, "Now you know who your neighbor is. It's anybody in need. Now you go, and be a neighbor to your neighbors. Love people like the Good Samaritan did. That's how God loves people."

All those involved in Jesus' parable had the assets and ability to assist their neighbor in need, but only one had the right attitude.

The Good Samaritan, a man probably used to being shunned himself because of his ethnicity, was a faithful steward.

# Ten Top Attitudes of Successful Stewards

The following ten attitudes are present in faithful managers of God's resources.

1. **Their motivation in life is love for God and people.**

   *'You shall love the Lord your God with all your heart, with all your soul,*
   *and with all your mind.' This is the great and foremost commandment.*
   *The second is like it. 'You shall love your neighbor as yourself.'*
   — Matthew 22:37-39

   *Owe nothing to anyone except to love one another; for he who loves his*
   *neighbor has fulfilled the law.*
   — Romans 13:8

2. **They live to give. They realize that giving is what living is all about.**

   *Give to him who asks of you, and do not turn away from him who wants*
   *to borrow from you.*
   — Matthew 5:42

   *Give, and it shall be given unto you; good measure, pressed down, shaken*
   *together, running over, they will pour into your lap. For by your standard*
   *of measure it will be measured to you in return.*
   — Luke 6:38

3. **They run to win, because they know life is a race to be run and won!**

   *Do you not know that those who run in a race all run, but only one*
   *receives the prize? Run in such a way that you may win.*
   — 1 Corinthians 9:24

   *Since we have so great a cloud of witnesses surrounding us, let us also lay*
   *aside every encumbrance, and the sin which so easily entangles us, and let*
   *us run with endurance the race that is set before us.*
   — Hebrews 12:1

4. **They are second-milers. They know extra effort is the edge that gets the job done.**

   *Whoever shall force you to go one mile, go with him two.*
   — Matthew 5:41

*Receive him (Epaphroditus) in the Lord with all joy, and hold men like*
*him in high regard; because he came close to death for the work of Christ,*
*risking his life to complete what was deficient in your service to me.*
— Philippians 2:29-30

5. **They are generous with God's resources. They know maximum giving results in maximum living.**

   *The generous man will be prosperous, and he who waters will himself*
   *be watered.*
   — Proverbs 11:25

   *He who is generous will be blessed, for he gives some of his food to the*
   *poor.*
   — Proverbs 22:9

6. **They apply the golden rule by treating others the same way they would like to be treated.**

   *However you want people to treat you, so treat them, for this is the Law*
   *and the Prophets.*
   — Matthew 7:12

   *A man that has friends must show himself friendly; and there is a friend*
   *that sticketh closer than a brother.*
   — Proverbs 18:24 KJV

7. **They are possibility thinkers. They have a positive outlook on life. They know that with God all things are possible. They believe the best is yet to come.**

   *'I know the plans that I have for you,' declares the Lord, 'plans for welfare*
   *and not for calamity to give you a future and a hope.'*
   — Jeremiah 29:11

   *Looking upon them Jesus said to them, 'With men this is impossible, but*
   *with God all things are possible.'*
   — Matthew 19:26

8. **They are faith-talking, faith-walking people. They trust God to meet their needs and use them to meet the needs of others.**

   *We walk by faith, not by sight.*
   — 2 Corinthians 5:7

*Faith is the assurance of things hoped for, the conviction of things not seen. For by it the men of old gained approval.*

— Hebrews 11:1-2

*Whatever is born of God overcomes the world; and this is the victory that has overcome the world — our faith.*

— 1 John 4:4

9. **They are finishers. They finish what they start. They end what they begin. They know the end of a matter is better than its beginning, and rewards go to those who finish**.

   *The end of a mater is better than its beginning, patience of spirit is better than arrogance of spirit.*

   — Ecclesiastes 7:7-8

   *I have fought the good fight, I have finished the course, I have kept the faith; in the future there is laid up for me the crown of righteousness, which the Lord, the righteous Judge, will award to me on that day; and not only to me, but also to all who have loved His appearing.*

   — 2 Timothy 4:7-8

10. **They are accountable. They live in the light of answering to the Lord for their management of His resources.**

    *Each one of us shall give an account of himself to God.*

    — Romans 14:12

    *They shall give account to Him who is ready to judge the living and the dead.*

    — 1 Peter 4:5

    *For this reason the kingdom of heaven may be compared to a certain king who wished to settle accounts with his slaves.*

    — Matthew 18:23

# Attitude Checklist

Evaluate your personal attitudes as a faithful steward. Then take your checklist and talk to God about it. Confess your failures and commit yourself, with His help, to success in the future.

| STEWARDSHIP ATTITUDE | ALWAYS | SOMETIMES | SELDOM |
|---|---|---|---|
| 1. Love God and People | _____ | _____ | _____ |
| 2. Live to Give | _____ | _____ | _____ |
| 3. Run to Win | _____ | _____ | _____ |
| 4. Second Miler | _____ | _____ | _____ |
| 5. Generous Giver | _____ | _____ | _____ |
| 6. Apply the Golden Rule | _____ | _____ | _____ |
| 7. Possibility Thinker | _____ | _____ | _____ |
| 8. Faith Talker/Walker | _____ | _____ | _____ |
| 9. Finisher | _____ | _____ | _____ |
| 10. Accountable | _____ | _____ | _____ |

# Are You Willing...

...to close the book of complaints and to open the book of praise?

...to believe other men are quite as sincere as you are and treat them with respect?

...to ignore what life owes you and to think about what you owe life?

...to stop looking for friendship and to start being friendly?

...to be content with such things as you have and to stop whining for the things you have not?

...to enjoy the simpler blessings and to cease striving for the artificial pleasures of the day?

...to cease looking for someone to help you and to devote yourself to helping others?

...to accept Jesus Christ as your Savior and to let your life be an outlet of His love, joy, and peace?

— *The Guide to Light*

# Lesson 5

## Hurdles to Prosperity and Successful Stewardship

*He did not do many miracles there because of their unbelief.*
— Matthew 13:58

PRINCIPLES
- God is not against His people being happy and blessed.
- God is no respecter of persons when it comes to blessing and success.
- People who don't believe in being prosperous, aren't!

PURPOSE
Successful stewardship and the accompanying blessings of prosperity are biblical benefits that belong to every born-again believer in Christ. Our purpose in this lesson will be twofold. First, to identify common hurdles to prosperity and "prosperity thieves" who seek to rob us of success. We will look at common obstacles and objections people have to being prosperous in this life. Second, we will share a simple how-to strategy for overcoming the obstacles to prosperity.

DISCUSSION
I was always the small kid in class. Our family genepool produced males built low to the ground. Even the giggly girls in elementary school made note of my shortness; they nicknamed me "Tiny." Now "Tiny" was cute from the innocent lips of the young ladies at school, but it wasn't so cute when the bigger boys used it to poke fun at me. Their mocking and taunting motivated me to prove to them that dynamite comes in small packages. I wanted so badly to show them what a little guy could do. I decided the sports venue would be my proving ground.

But my unbridled enthusiasm for sports wasn't enough. I had to face facts. Being short did prove problematic when it came to playing basketball. I was also too small for football, and I didn't have a lot of swinging power at the plate for baseball. So, I determined to make my mark in the athletic world on the track field. For obvious reasons, the high jump was out. My legs were too short for sprints and long distance races. But one event did attract my attention.

The hurdles.

Successful stewardship and the accompanying blessings of prosperity are biblical benefits that belong to every born-again believer in Christ.

Tryouts for the track team took place in early spring. When the coach wanted to know what I would like to audition for I yelled, "Hurdles, sir!" I had never run hurdles before, but I was more than willing to give them a shot! The coach asked if I preferred high or low hurdles. Being "Tiny," low hurdles sounded good to me, so without hesitation, I confidently replied that the low hurdles would be just right.

The first time I ran hurdles, I fell head and heels over the very first one! Running full-speed ahead, I leapt over the hurdle, hit the top with my track shoe, and thudded to the ground! I scraped my hands, bruised my knees, and shattered my ego on the asphalt track. The other hurdlers ran into the sunset to glory, crossing the finish line as I lay in my lane.

I was embarrassed. I felt like quitting; maybe hurdles weren't for me, after all. But I knew better. Though I had lost round one, these frustrating roadblocks were obstacles to overcome. I studied the style of the more experienced hurdlers, received helpful pointers from the coach, and with lots of good old practice, I learned to leap over those hurdles successfully.

My elementary track career? "Tiny" never set any records. Olympic gold was certainly not in my future! I did earn a third place ribbon once. But my most memorable accomplishment was this: I overcame the hurdles, and in doing so, I also learned that physical stature does not make the man — heart and character do.

> My most memorable accomplishment was this: I overcame the hurdles, and in doing so, I also learned that physical stature does not make the man — heart and character do.

## Prosperity: God's Plan for Man?

Is prosperity and success God's plan for man, or isn't it? Before we proceed, look up and study the following scripture references on prosperity.

| | | |
|---|---|---|
| Psalm 35: 7-28 | Psalm 37:11 | Proverbs 28:25 |
| Proverbs 10: 15-16 | Proverbs 11:28 | Proverbs 3:13-14 |
| Proverbs 37:25 | Proverbs 22:9 | 3 John 2 |
| Luke 6:38 | 2 Corinthians 8:1-2 | Proverbs 16:20 |
| 1 Corinthians 9:6-8 | Proverbs 4:5-13 | Matthew 6:25-33 |
| Proverbs 13:4 | Genesis 39:2 | Genesis 24:21 |
| Genesis 12:1-3 | Romans 1:10 | Psalm 107:33-38 |
| Psalm 122:6-7 | Psalm 13:4 | Joshua 1:1-9 |

Summarize what these passages from God's Word say about prosperity and success.

_____

_____

_____

_____

_____

_____

_____

Now, from your personal study, do you believe prosperity is God's plan for man?

_____

_____

_____

_____

_____

Peter writes in Acts 10:34-35:

> Opening his mouth Peter said, "I most certainly understand that God is
> not one to show partiality (is no respecter of persons). But in every nation,
> the man who fears Him and does what is right is welcome to Him.

According to Peter's words, for whom is God's promise?

_____

_____

_____

_____

If you believe prosperity is God's will for you, how do these promises apply to your life?

_____

_____

_____

_____

_____

_____

## IMPORTANT POINT TO PONDER

Prosperity is not automatic. Obstacles, objections and opposition have always stood between God's people and God's promises. Anything worthwhile or worth having will be contested. It's a fact of life. In this life, nothing of enduring value ever comes easily, either. The prizes that God promises for successful stewardship come with much faith and lots of hard work!

High hurdles and low hurdles will always obstruct our way to prosperity and God's blessing. The way we handle the hurdles to prosperity determines success or failure in our stewardship race.

# Obstacles Are Meant to Be Overcome

The word *salvation* in Scripture comes from the Greek word soteria, which denotes deliverance, preservation, wholeness, and wellness in every area of life. While in bondage to sin, mankind was unhealthy in spirit, body, and soul. People were hopelessly lost and unable to save themselves. God, through Jesus Christ, did something about man's problem. He redeemed His people from the curse of the Law.

> *Christ redeemed us from the curse of the Law, having become a curse for us*
> *— for it is written, "Cursed is everyone who hangs on a tree" — in order that*
> *in Christ Jesus the blessing of Abraham might come to the Gentiles, so that we*
> *might receive the promise of the Spirit through faith.*
> — Galatians 3:13-14

The "curse of the Law" is found in Deuteronomy 28:15-68. These fifty-four verses can be summed up under three main headings: the curses of sickness, poverty and death. Jesus, by His atoning death at Calvary, redeemed us, or bought us back, from the consequences of disobeying God's law. His sacrifice provided health, prosperity, and eternal life for all who believe in Him.

Spiritual, relational, mental, emotional, physical, financial, and material prosperity is our inheritance through Christ. God's plan and purpose is for His people to prosper. Prosperity is made possible by Christ's provision of salvation on the Cross.

Think about this: A person living under a curse cannot be blessed; a person who is cursed cannot be a blessing to others.

Spiritual, relational, mental, emotional, physical, financial, and material prosperity is our inheritance through Christ. God's plan and purpose is for His people to prosper. Prosperity is made possible by Christ's provision of salvation on the Cross.

A prosperous lifestyle is biblical. It belongs to all who pursue it with faith and who practice obedience to the prosperity principles taught in the Word.

# A Promise for Prosperity: Joshua 1:1-9

At a pivotal point in Israel's history, God reaffirmed His position on prosperity. Moses had died. Joshua was elevated to senior leader. Moses' apprentice and chief understudy for forty years would now lead the Jewish nation into the Promised Land.

The Lord knew Joshua might feel a bit overwhelmed with his promotion and significant responsibilities. It was an awesome task before him, so God assured Joshua of success. In verses 1-6, God told Joshua he could arise, with confidence, and cross the Jordan with all the people. God gave Joshua the following reasons to hope for victory and success.

| | |
|---|---|
| God had already given Israel the land. | vv. 2-3 |
| Every place they put their foot would be theirs. | vv. 3-4 |
| No man would withstand them all their life. | v. 5 |
| God would be with Joshua just as He was with Moses. | v. 5 |
| God would not fail Joshua or forsake him. | v. 5 |

The Lord was with Israel and would always be with them. He had secured the land for them and would never let His children down.

God reassured Joshua that He would be there to do His part. Just as He had been with Moses, so Almighty God would be with Joshua.

But Joshua would have to do His part. God commanded Joshua to "be strong and courageous" (vv. 6, 9). This mission wasn't for a weak, cowardly man. For Joshua, God would give them possession of the land. God had already given it to them in the spiritual realm. Joshua would actually deliver it to them in the natural realm.

In order to be successful, Joshua had to be very careful to follow God's instructions. Verses 7-9 contain the critical keys to Joshua's personal success and ultimate prosperity in the Promised Land.

Only be strong and courageous, be careful to do according to all the law which Moses My servant commanded you; do not turn from it to the right or to the left, so that you may have success wherever you go.

At a pivotal point in Israel's history, God reaffirmed His position on prosperity. Moses had died. Joshua was elevated to senior leader. Moses' apprentice and chief understudy for forty years would now lead the Jewish nation into the Promised Land.

This book of the law shall not depart from your mouth, but you shall meditate on it day and night, to do according to all that is written in it; for then you shall make your way prosperous, and then you will have success.

Have I not commanded you? Be strong and courageous! Do not tremble or be dismayed, for the Lord your God is with you wherever you go.

Joshua's part in this divine/human partnership was mapped out very clearly. He was to focus on four priorities.

- He was "to do" (obey) all of God's law and not deviate from it in anyway. (v. 7)
- God's law was to always be in Joshua's mouth. He was to refer to and speak the Word continually. (v. 8)
- Joshua was to meditate (chew over) the Word twenty-four hours a day. (v. 8)
- He was not to tremble or be disheartened in anyway. God was with him (v. 9)

Prosperity and success was not only up to God. It was also up to Joshua. He had to meet the conditions. It was his choice to obey the Word or not, meditate on God's promises or not, stick to the law of God or not. If Joshua did those things, he would prosper and succeed. If not, he would fail.

NOTE
God said that when Joshua did the above things, then his way would be made prosperous. He would have success wherever he went. Also note the phrase in verse 8:

"Then_____make_____prosperous and then ___
_____ have success."

After reviewing verse 8, who do you think was ultimately responsible for Joshua's prosperity and success? _____

It's vitally important to see here that Joshua would make his way prosperous and experience personal success — when he did what God told him to do.

Prosperity and success was not only up to God. It was also up to Joshua. He had to meet the conditions. It was his choice to obey the Word or not, meditate on God's promises or not, stick to the law of God or not. If Joshua did those things, he would prosper and succeed. If not, he would fail.

Joshua was appointed and anointed to be a faithful steward of God's Word. He was to manage God's people and resources according to the principles stated in the Word of God.

In God's Kingdom, we must do our part if we are to prosper and be successful.

# Hurdles to Prosperity

Today many people trip over the hurdles to God's promises of prosperity and success. They find it difficult to believe, let alone achieve, the levels of success the Lord has ordained for His people.

Two primary sources of opposition become hurdles in the pathway of prosperity.

Satan is number one. The devil knows the Word, hates the Word, and does his best to steal the promises of the Word from God's people. John 8:44 and 10:10 describe the essential nature, character (actually lack of!), and method of operation of Satan.

You (speaking of the Pharisees) are of your father the devil, and you want to do the desires of your father. He was a murderer from the beginning, and does not stand in the truth, because there is no truth in him. Whenever he speaks a lie, he speaks from his own nature; for he is a liar and the father of lies....

The thief comes only to steal, kill, and destroy.

Satan is a lying, murdering thief, who steals, kills, and destroys. (Not a nice guy.) Yet it is amazing how many people listen to his lying voice.

There is no truth in the devil. The evil one is one big lie! He spins seductive lies to unsuspecting people about God's promises to prosper them. He is a dirty dog who seeks to steal any thought of success from their spirits. Satan's goal is to dash and destroy all dreams and hopes for success in this life.

Here's how Satan lies:
He suggests to you that God's Word is false — a myth or a fairy tale. A nice story, but not to be believed. He whispers that God really isn't a good God and He doesn't want to give you good things. After all, Satan says, when was the last time God did anything good for you?

He might say you're struggling to pay your bills right now; where is God and His prosperity and success when you really need Him? If God is so committed to your personal success, why did you lose your job? Think about that! Are you sure He cares about you and your family? That non-Christian family down the street is doing great. New home and furniture. New cars. They're prospering without believing in the Bible. Where does that leave you?

> The devil knows the Word, hates the Word, and does his best to steal the promises of the Word from God's people.

Don't buy into that that tithing, giving, and serving stuff. It just leaves you with less. Givers don't gain, they lose. How will you ever get ahead if you give your money and time away to others? It doesn't seem right, does it, to give away what is yours? All the church and those greedy preachers want is your money, Spend it on yourself. You earned it. Nobody helped you.

Lies, lies, lies and more lies. Straight from the pit of hell!

Through his lying tactics and destructive spiritual attacks, the devil purposefully creates confusion, frustration, and despair in people. And Christians are not exempt from his subtle, but very real attacks. They are especially vulnerable when they neglect to mediate day and night upon God's Word as Joshua was told to do.

If you forget to study the Word and by faith, stand on its "precious and magnificent promises" (1 Peter 1:2-4), be certain Satan will find you and get in your face.

Satan becomes a somewhat formidable, but not unbeatable spiritual hurdle on the road to biblical prosperity. Never forget: He's defeated! Jesus defeated him on a Cross and at an empty tomb! Because of Him (Jesus) we win over him (the devil). The Word says, in 1 John 3:8, that the Son of God appeared for this purpose, that He might (and He did!) destroy the works of the devil. And in 1 John 4:4, "You are from God, little children, and have overcome them; for greater is He (Jesus) who is in you than he (Satan) who is in the world."

Christians always overcome Satan when they stand up to him in the name of Jesus Christ of Nazareth!

If you listen to the lies of the devil, you will never believe that it is God's plan to prosper you. If you don't believe it, you will never receive it. You will never know success in Christ if you succumb to the evil schemes and deceitful trickery of Satan.

## COMMIT TO THIS PLAN OF ACTION

These are the steps I will take the next time Satan lies and tries to steal God's blessings from me.

1. **I will not listen to the voice of the devil.**
   *When he puts forth all his own, he goes before them, and the sheep follow him because they know his voice. And a stranger they simply will not follow, but will flee from him, because they do not know the voice of strangers.*
   — John 10:4-5

2. **I will rebuke and resist the evil one by faith in Jesus name.**

   *Submit therefore to God. Resist the devil and he will flee from you.*
   — James 4:7

   *Be of sober spirit, be on the alert. Your adversary, the devil, prowls about like a roaring lion, seeking some to devour. But resist him, firm in your faith, knowing that the same experiences of suffering are being accomplished by your brethren who are in the world. And after you have suffered for a little while, the God of all grace, who called you to His eternal glory in Christ, will Himself, perfect, confirm, strengthen, and establish you.*
   — 1 Peter 5:8-10

3. **I will stand firm on God' promises of prosperity for me.**

   *Put on the full armor of God, that you may be able to stand firm against the schemes of the devil. For our struggle is not against flesh and blood, but against rulers, against the powers, against the world forces of this darkness, against the spiritual forces of wickedness in the heavenly places. Therefore, take up the full armor of God, that you may be able to resist in the evil day, and having done everything, to stand firm.*
   — Ephesians 6:11-13

4. **I will rejoice, that in Christ, I always triumph over the devil!**

   *Thanks be to God, who always leads us in triumph in Christ, and manifests through us the sweet aroma of the knowledge of Him in every place.*
   — 2 Corinthians 2:14

   *They overcame him (Satan) because of the blood of the Lamb and because of the word of their testimony.*
   — Revelation 12:11

# Prosperity Thieves

Satan is, without doubt, the chief hurdle to prosperity. He is the ultimate prosperity thief and is the father of all prosperity thieves. This lying, thieving father has produced a number of menacing, intimidating children. Satan's anti-prosperity offspring erect strongholds in the minds of people to keep them from experiencing God's blessings.

The second major source that produces hurdles to prosperity is man and his thinking. We ourselves, and others are often guilty of placing significant hurdles in the path of prosperity. These conscious and unconscious obstacles can trip people up and rob them of prosperity and success.

Let's examine five significant prosperity thieves that seek to steal success from our lives.

## THIEF #1: Doubt and Unbelief

Have you ever heard people make statements like these: "I just can't buy into that prosperity teaching. It's just a bunch of wishful thinking!" "Prosperity is just too good to be true." "I can't believe that God wants me to be successful." "I believe Jesus is my Savior, and God will heal my sick body, but I really doubt if He wants me to live in a nice home, drive a new automobile, wear nice clothes, have money in the bank, or have extra to give to needy people." "Success for Christians? Not in this life!" "Prosperity might be for others, but I'm sure it is not for me."

Have you ever spoken these words yourself?

Maybe you have. Many well-intentioned, professing Christians do. These all-too-common misconceptions concerning biblical prosperity are expressed by people who have believed Satan's lie that God doesn't want them to prosper. Whether they know it or not, they have been robbed! Thieves take what rightfully belongs to others. These individuals' biblical blessings have been stolen. The thief of doubt and unbelief has picked their spiritual pockets!

God's Kingdom, overall, operates on this one profound principle: Believe and receive or doubt and do without!

This foundational principle can be seen in the following three key areas of life.

1. Man can't receive salvation until he believes in the Savior. John 1:12 tells us as many as received Him, to them He gave the right to become children of God, even to those who believe in His name. If you want to become a child of God, first believe in Jesus, then receive Jesus. Unbelief leaves a person unsaved. Belief leads to being born-again into the Kingdom of God.

2. Sick people don't receive healing until they first believe in the healing power of Jesus Christ. In the Gospel of Mark, chapter 5, verses 22-24, and 35-43, we find the record of Jesus healing (raising from the dead!) Jairus' daughter. A well-known official of the Jewish synagogue came to Jesus because his little girl

> If you want to become a child of God, first believe in Jesus, then receive Jesus. Unbelief leaves a person unsaved. Belief leads to being born-again into the Kingdom of God.

was dying. This desperate, but believing daddy requested, "My little daughter is at the point of death; please come and lay your hands on her, that she may get well and live."

Jairus had faith that Jesus could and would heal his daughter. On the way to Jairus' home, a huge crowd of needy people detained the Lord. Verses 23-34 record the remarkable account of how He healed a woman who had suffered with an incurable disease for over twelve years. Jesus said to her, "Daughter, your faith has made you well; go in peace and be healed of your affliction" (v. 34). This precious woman's faith, her personal belief in Jesus, healed her disease.

During the delay, word came that the little girl had died. Jairus' servants delivered the sad news and suggested their master not trouble the Teacher anymore. Read Jesus' challenging response to the official:

> *Jesus, overhearing what was being spoken, said to the synagogue official. 'Do not be afraid any longer, only believe!'*
> — Mark 5:36

Jairus, listen to me. I know the news is bad. But I have good news for you. She is not dead, only asleep. Facts are facts, but faith changes facts. Kick out fear and fire up your faith. The issue of this hour, at this critical moment, Jairus, is to believe. Only believe. Don't doubt or fear. I am here. Watch me do a miracle for you and your little girl.

The healing miracle takes place in verses 37-43.

Jesus took Peter, James, John, and Jairus and his wife — all believers —, into the room. He threw the weeping, mocking, laughing unbelievers out. With the believers inside and the doubters outside, Jesus spoke to the girl. She rose immediately, walking away from her sick/death bed in perfect health! Everyone who witnessed this miracle was completely astounded.

Jairus believed and his little helpless daughter received.

3. People don't receive prosperity until they first believe that it is God's will for them to prosper. Prosperity and success isn't any different than salvation, healing, or any of the other covenant blessings of the Kingdom. They all require faith — believing before receiving.

Mark 9:23 declares that "all things are possible to him who believes." biblical prosperity is included in the "all things" Jesus mentioned. But prosperity is not possible unless one believes.

Unbelief hinders the power of God. Lack of faith holds back every good blessing God wants to give to His children. It's a spiritual hurdle to salvation, healing and prosperity. Matthew 13:53-58 shows us just how powerful unbelief can be.

Jesus went home to Nazareth, but His homecoming was less than glorious! As was the Lord's custom, He taught the Word in the local synagogue. Some of His listeners were astonished. Others were deeply offended. They rejected His authority and wisdom because they couldn't get past the fact that the Son of God was the son of a local carpenter. He was of human stock, so how in the world could He teach this way? How could He be divine?

Jesus tried to perform some miracles, but wasn't very successful.

Study verse 58. What prevented Jesus from doing "many miracles" in front of the hometown people?

_____
_____
_____

The problem? "Because of their unbelief." Miraculous healings were hindered, not because of these people's inability to believe, or their lack of opportunity to believe, but simply because they chose not to believe. They doubted Jesus could heal. And guess what: They received exactly what they believed God for.

Believe and receive or doubt and do without!

Belief or Unbelief? The bottom line concerning whether or not you are a candidate for prosperity is this: Do you believe that God will prosper you?

> Unbelief hinders the power of God. Lack of faith holds back every good blessing God wants to give to His children. It's a spiritual hurdle to salvation, healing and prosperity.

## SELF-EXAMINATION

1. Regarding biblical prosperity and success, do you consider yourself a believer or an unbeliever?

   _____

   _____

   _____

2. Do you doubt God's promise to prosper you? If so, why do you doubt His promise?

   _____

   _____

   _____

   _____

3. Do you have faith for prosperity?

   _____

   _____

   _____

4. When it comes to God's blessings, would those who know you best say you are a person who believes and receives, or one who doubts and does without?

   _____

   _____

   _____

   _____

   _____

I choose to be prosperous and successful in this life. I will not allow the thief of doubt and unbelief to steal the prosperity that belongs to me! By faith, I declare with my mouth that I believe in biblical prosperity.

## CONFESSION OF FAITH

I choose to be prosperous and successful in this life. I will not allow the thief of doubt and unbelief to steal the prosperity that belongs to me! By faith, I declare with my mouth that I believe in biblical prosperity. If I wrestle with doubt, I will honestly seek the Lord and ask Him to help my unbelief. I trust God to help me turn unbelief into belief.

## THIEF #2: Poverty Theology

Like many Christians, I was raised in a denominational setting that did not believe in prosperity. Doctrinally, they confessed a creed that says God will take care of our needs. But when it came to actually believing and trusting Him for the prosperity and success that will allow a Christian to not only be blessed but also bless others, they fell far short of what Scripture says.

Over and over again I heard words from my spiritual elders who were either ignorant of, misunderstood, or in fact resisted God's promise to bless their lives.

- Man is not worthy of great blessing from God.
- We are just lowly sinners who don't deserve to be blessed.
- If it is God's will, He will bless us.
- If God chooses to bless someone that's fine, but prosperity isn't a promise for everyone.
- Christians stay humble when they are poor.
- God's people learn valuable lessons about godliness and Christ-like character when they have to do without and depend on Him to meet their needs.
- Christians are saved from this world, so we shouldn't be rich in the things of the world. How can we be a true Christian and be wealthy?

Have you ever heard this noble-sounding, non-scriptural rhetoric? It sounds religious, respectable, doctrinally sound, and personally reassuring — if you see yourself as a lowly worm that serves a stingy heavenly Father who doesn't really want to do anything good for you.

These religious positions reflect a "worm" theology and a poverty or "poor me" mindset.

The lowly worm view of man comes from Job 25:6 and Psalm 22:6. But if you make a careful study of these scriptures in their entire context, you will come to the obvious conclusion: God is not in any way declaring that man is a worm, or less than a worm.

In the passage in Job, Bildad, one of Job's friends and comforters, tells Job that sin and wrongdoing are the reason for his suffering. That was not the case. The Lord Himself (in Job 1:8) describes His servant Job as a blameless, upright man, fearing God and turning away from evil. According to his Maker, there was no righteous man like Job on all of planet earth. Job had God's seal of approval!

Bildad misread and misunderstood Job's situation, thinking his friend was proud and covering evil in his life. He was certain that somehow, in some way, Job had surely exalted himself against the Almighty. In trying to teach Job a lesson on

When it came to actually believing and trusting Him for the prosperity and success that will allow a Christian to not only be blessed but also bless others, they fell far short of what Scripture says.

the humble nature of man in light of the awesomeness of Almighty God, Bildad only used the term "worm" as a word picture to describe the wide difference between man and his Maker. There is a greatness gap between Creator and creature. But Bildad did not ascribe worminess to man as his essential nature.

In Psalm 22:1-8, the reference is prophetic, looking forward to Christ's agonizing death at Calvary. Because of the mocking, jeering, and sneering of men toward the Lord as He hung on the Cross, Jesus became a reproach to men. Unbelieving men tortured and taunted Jesus, treating Him in a manner less than an ordinary man would be treated. More like a worm.

But the psalmist did not make a dogmatic, doctrinal declaration and say that man is no better than a worm. And while hanging on the Cross, Jesus, in word and deed, did not act like a worm. He conducted Himself like a champion!

Jesus did not die for worms! He died for precious human beings. It is not His will that even one man or woman, boy or girl perish (2 Peter 3:9). Jesus' sacrificial death and triumphant resurrection from the dead provide eternal salvation. He adopts His "saints" into the divine family, calling them His brothers and sisters, making them joint-heirs with Him of all the riches of the Kingdom of God.

Read Romans 8:14-17, Galatians 3:29, Galatians 4:7, Titus 3:7, Hebrews 1:14, Hebrews 6:17, Ephesians 1:18, Acts 20:32, Acts 26:18, Colossians 1:12, and 1 Peter 1:3-4. Do these scriptures support a poverty theology?

---

Christ's inheritance is our inheritance. He is not poor, nor are we. God's children are rich in Him!

Unfortunately, some Christians want to believe that they are to be poor all of their lives. They see poverty as a sacred and honorable virtue, a holy and humble calling, that somehow makes us more godly. To them, being a have-not in this world is more glorious and God-like than being a person who has things.

If you have ever thought that poverty is a blessing in any way, seriously consider the following six questions.

1. List your scriptural proof that God blesses poverty. Show where in the Word it says that God is the source of poverty.

   _____

   _____

   _____

   _____

2. Explain the hundreds of Old and New Testament scriptures that promise prosperity and success to God's people.

   _____

   _____

   _____

   _____

3. If you have ever been poor, did the sting of poverty feel good or godly to you? What advantages do the poor have? How does this world treat the poor?

   _____

   _____

   _____

   _____

   _____

   _____

4. Why would the good God of the Bible want His children to be poor and suffer the inhumane indignities that accompany poverty?

   _____

   _____

   _____

   _____

   _____

   _____

5. If you are poor, how can you help others escape the self-esteem shattering bondage of poverty?

   _____

   _____

   _____

   _____

6. If you are not blessed, how can you bless someone else?

_____

_____

_____

_____

_____

_____

People are not worms. Poverty is not God's will for people. In light of the long list of blessings and benefits promised to God's people recorded in Deuteronomy 28:1-14, a poverty mindset is an invention of man, not inspiration from God:

> It shall be if you shall diligently obey the Lord your God, being careful to do all His commandments which I command you today, the Lord your God will set you high above all the nations of the earth. And all these blessings shall come upon you and overtake you, if you will obey the Lord your God. Blessed shall you be in the city, and blessed shall you be in the country. Blessed shall be the offspring of your body and the produce of your ground and the offspring of your beasts, and the increase of your herd and the young of your flock. Blessed shall be your basket and your kneading bowl. Blessed shall you be when you come in, and blessed shall you be when you go out. The Lord will cause your enemies who rise up against you to be defeated before you; they shall come up against you one way and shall flee before you seven ways. The Lord will command the blessing upon you in your barns and in all that you put your hand to, and He will bless you in the land which the Lord your God gives you. The Lord will establish you as a holy people to Himself, as He swore to you, if you will keep the commandments of the Lord your God, and walk in His ways. So all the peoples of the earth shall see that you are called by the name of the Lord, and they shall be afraid of you. And the Lord will make you abound in prosperity, in the offspring of your body and in the offspring of your beast and in the produce of your ground, in the land which the Lord swore to your fathers to give you. The Lord will open for you His good storehouse, the heavens, to give rain to your land in its season and to bless all the work of your hand; and you shall lend to many nations, and shall not borrow. And the Lord will make you the head, and not the tail, and you only shall be above, and you shall not be underneath, if you will listen to the commandments of the Lord your God, which I charge you today, to observe them carefully. And do not turn aside from any of the words which I command you today, to the right or to the left, to go after other gods to serve them.

Poverty is not God's will for people. In light of the long list of blessings and benefits promised to God's people recorded in Deuteronomy 28:1-14, a poverty mindset is an invention of man, not inspiration from God.

## SUMMARY

God's covenant people are blessed wherever they are, wherever they go, and in whatever they do. They experience and enjoy abundance in every area of life. Victory over enemies belongs to them. They're the head, not the tail in life; always above, never beneath. As long as they listen to Him, obey His Word, and serve Him all the days of their lives, God will always be with them and for them, working on their behalf to prosper them and make them successful.

Sounds like a prosperous and successful lifestyle to me! What do you think?

_____
_____
_____
_____
_____
_____
_____
_____
_____

Poverty theology can rob you of the blessings and benefits of the promises of prosperity.

God's covenant people are blessed wherever they are, wherever they go, and in whatever they do. They experience and enjoy abundance in every area of life. Victory over enemies belongs to them.

## PERSONAL APPLICATION

List areas of your life where you may have been infected with a poverty mindset.

_____
_____
_____

Who or what was the source of your poverty theology?

_____
_____
_____
_____
_____
_____
_____

How has poverty theology kept you from prospering?

_____

_____

_____

_____

_____

What have you lost because of a poor-me mindset?

_____

_____

_____

_____

_____

_____

_____

What could you gain by changing your theology from poverty to prosperity?

_____

_____

_____

_____

_____

_____

God, help me renew my mind through the Word of God and change my attitudes and behavior concerning prosperity.

## PERSONAL PRAYER

Heavenly Father, I come to You to confess that I have been hindered by poverty theology in the past. Starting today, I desire to go into the future by faith, trusting in Your Word that prosperity and success is for me. Help me renew my mind through the Word of God and change my attitudes and behavior concerning prosperity. Thank You for helping me straighten out my theology in this area. In Jesus' name, amen.

# Lesson 6

## More Hurdles to Prosperity and Successful Stewardship

*The thief comes only to steal, kill and destroy: I (Jesus) came that they might have life, and might have it abundantly.*
— John 10:10

### PRINCIPLES

- The power of God's Word overpowers and overcomes prosperity thieves.
- Successful stewards have overcome the obstacles to prosperity.
- Prosperity and success become yours the moment you begin to believe!

### DISCUSSION
## More Prosperity Thieves

### THIEF #3: Unbiblical Prosperity

Let's say we are taking a trip to another city by automobile. Our journey begins with high expectations. We look forward to enjoying a nice, uneventful ride to our destination. Along the way, we become distracted, take our eyes off the highway, swerve off the road, and drive our car into a ditch alongside the roadway. Our scenic trip comes to a screeching halt.

So there we are, stuck in a ditch. We can't get very far down the road like that. Just try driving in a ditch and see how far you travel. All you do is tear up your car and get nowhere.

If we are to arrive safely and successfully to our destination, we must steer our car down the middle of our lane. Good drivers must stay awake and alert at all times, must focus on the changing road conditions, avoid inevitable distractions, and stay out of the ditches on both sides of the highway.

Ditches are dangerous. Automakers did not design automobiles to operate in ditches. Deep ruts in the dirt will definitely stop your forward progress in a hurry! Cars were created to cruise smoothly down level roadbeds, not crash into ditches.

Ditches and prosperity. What in the world do they have to do with one another, anyway?

The power of God's Word overpowers and overcomes prosperity thieves.

We must avoid two distinct theological ditches when it comes to prosperity. Some Christians become distracted and run off the road into poverty theology. We have already discussed how discouraging a "poor-me" mindset is and the damage it can do.

This is dangerous. It causes people to miss God's abundant blessings because they think He wants them to be poor.

Other believers swerve their theology another direction and run off the road in the opposite direction. They avoid the poverty issue only to drive straight into unbiblical prosperity.

This is equally as dangerous. It causes God's people to bypass God's richest blessings because they think that He only wants them to be financially rich.

As you journey through life, you must remain alert and avoid both of these deadly theological ditches. Either will prevent you from experiencing the true blessings of biblical prosperity. These diametrically opposite, but equally dangerous theologies are detrimental to the mature development of a Christ-like, Bible-based understanding of lifestyle stewardship.

## What Is Unbiblical Prosperity?

This erroneous teaching is an extreme view of prosperity that is biblically out of balance and out of bounds. Some preachers and teachers in the body of Christ today have gone overboard regarding prosperity. They have crossed a fine line in the Word. According to them, prosperity is narrowly defined to mean financial wealth. The broader, biblical concept of prosperity — as a total lifestyle of well-being and thriving in our body, spirit, and soul — is sacrificed on the altar of material success (wealth).

They distort the scriptures in God's Word regarding prosperity to support this popular, excess-laden position. According to this teaching, prosperity equals wealth. Success becomes confused with excess. They teach that God's promises are His guarantees to untold financial and material abundance. Life is prosperous only when you can boast of a large financial portfolio.

This position disregards the sound wisdom and safe boundaries of biblical blessing.

Some preachers and teachers in the body of Christ today have gone overboard regarding prosperity. They have crossed a fine line in the Word. According to them, prosperity is narrowly defined to mean financial wealth. The broader, biblical concept of prosperity — as a total lifestyle of well-being and thriving in our body, spirit, and soul — is sacrificed on the altar of material success (wealth).

# What Does Unbiblical Prosperity Propose?

Simply stated: This popular unscriptural teaching says you haven't prospered unless you are wealthy. Proponents of this theology equate being rich with being prosperous. They promote financial wealth as the sole indicator of success. They say you can have anything and everything you want, when you want it, in the way you want it. Name it and claim it, and it's yours.

The goal of unbiblical prosperity is financial gain. In this unscriptural system, the concept of having faith for finances borders on presumption. God is presumed to be at our disposal to prosper us on our terms, not His. All we have to do is ask with faith, and God is obligated to give it to us. Wealth is the one sure sign of having arrived in the Promised Land of prosperity.

But is that biblically correct? Or is there more to prosperity than just material wealth?

Scripture certainly tells the true tales of wealthy men like Abraham, Job, Joseph, David, Solomon, Zaccheus, and the rich young ruler, just to name a few. Jesus, Himself, told parables about people with vast financial means. The Lord also managed a sizable amount of worldly wealth in order to carry out His ministry and support his staff of dedicated disciples and their families. The apostle Paul even addressed the perils of rich people (in 1 Timothy).

Money and wealth are part of prosperity, but not the only part. There is much more to prosperity than mere money. Proverbs 23:4-5 puts the pursuit of wealth purely for wealth's sake into proper perspective.

> Do not weary yourself to gain wealth, cease from your consideration of it. When you set your eyes on it, it is gone. For wealth certainly makes itself wings. Like an eagle that flies toward the heavens.

Solomon, who was one of the richest men the world has ever seen, (See 1 Kings 3:6-14.), issued a clear warning to seekers of wealth: Don't wear yourself out to just make money. Stop spending all your thought, time, and energy consumed with how you can become rich. Wealth itself is not life's reward. The moment money comes within your reach it flies away. Like an eagle, wealth spreads its wide wings, heads into the wind and soars high above your grasp. Gone. Just like that.

The goal of **unbiblical** prosperity is financial gain. In this unscriptural system, the concept of having faith for finances borders on presumption. God is presumed to be at our disposal to prosper us on our terms, not His. All we have to do is ask with faith, and God is obligated to give it to us. Wealth is the one sure sign of having arrived in the Promised Land of prosperity.

We saw in Deuteronomy 28:1-2 how Moses told the Israelites that if they obeyed and served the Lord, He would set them above the nations. True prosperity in every sense would be theirs. In verse two, the Word reads: And all these blessings shall come upon you and overtake you, if you will obey the Lord your God.

Moses was letting God's people in on a Kingdom secret. Don't chase wealth; let wealth chase you. Blessing and prosperity will find you if you obey the Lord. God's blessings will overtake you (literally, hunt, run down, overcome).

The prophet's emphasis is on obedience to God's Word. Put your energy into obeying the Lord, he says. Don't exhaust yourself chasing wealth. Let prosperity overtake you. God knows how to get His blessings to people who are obedient to His Word.

If you obey the Lord, the blessing of the Lord will overtake you.

Nearly three millennia later, the writings of the Apostle Paul echo Solomon's sentiment regarding the temporary nature of material riches. Putting riches into two categories, uncertain and certain, Paul instructs the young pastor Timothy to teach the rich where the real riches in life lie.

> *Instruct those who are rich in this present world not to be conceited or to fix their hope on the uncertainty of riches; but on God, who richly supplies us with all things. Instruct them to do good, to be rich in good works, to be generous and ready to share, storing up for themselves the treasure of a good foundation for the future, so that they may take hold of that which is life indeed.*
> — 1 Timothy 6:17-19

If you are rich, don't be proud and get a big ego because you are rich. Do not fasten your hope on uncertain riches that can be here today and gone tomorrow. Instead, fix your attention on God, who is the source of your wealth. Trust Him to supply you with the worldly riches you need to be successful.

If you really want to be rich do this. Focus on using your riches to enrich others' lives. Pursue more than money. Bless others with your blessings. Do good things for people. Be rich in good works. Be known as a generous person. Always be prepared to share your wealth with the less fortunate. When you do this, then you will take hold of what life is really all about — servanthood and stewardship. Then your riches will be true, certain riches. Real wealth, wealth you can count on, is laid up in heaven's storehouse.

If you are rich, don't be proud and get a big ego because you are rich. Do not fasten your hope on uncertain riches that can be here today and gone tomorrow. Instead, fix your attention on God, who is the source of your wealth.

# Unbiblical Prosperity Is Unbalanced

The Christian life is all about balance. The Bible is a balanced book. It never endorses extreme positions. Every doctrinal position is balanced by others. God's Word continually exhorts believers to walk straight and not veer to the right or to the left in life. The Word of God guides us and directs our paths to stay on the road and avoid ditches.

> *Let your eyes look directly ahead, and let your gaze be fixed straight in front of you. Watch the path of your feet, and all your ways will be established. Do not turn to the right or to the left; turn your foot from evil.*
> — Proverbs 4:25-27

Prosperity is a well-balanced doctrine with many important components. Prosperity is a complete package of biblical issues that contribute to the entirety of a prosperous lifestyle. There is no whole without all of the parts.

Overdue and undue emphasis on the material and financial side of success and prosperity neglects the other aspects of a fully balanced lifestyle of prosperity.

## CONSIDER THIS

Imbalanced, unbiblical prosperity must come to terms with the following components of a prosperous lifestyle. Do or don't these issues fit into the promises of prosperity we have in the Bible?

1. Physical health and emotional well-being?
2. Mutually satisfying personal relationships?
3. Sacrificial giving of our time to help others become successful?
4. Using and managing our God-given natural gifts and talents for His glory and the good of men?
5. Where does favor with God and men fit into the prosperity picture?
6. Does the successful stewardship or our testimony of salvation contribute to a prosperous life? Does soul-winning have anything to do with being prosperous?
7. What part does leaving a Christian legacy to our children and grandchildren play in the overall plan of prosperity?

Prosperity is a well-balanced doctrine with many important components. Prosperity is a complete package of biblical issues that contribute to the entirety of a prosperous lifestyle. There is no whole without all of the parts.

*Thus says the Lord, "Let not a wise man boast of his wisdom, and let not the mighty man boast of his might, let not a rich man boast of his riches; but let him who boasts, boast of this that he understands and knows Me, that I am the Lord, who exercises lovingkindness, justice and righteousness on earth; for I delight in these things, declares the Lord."*
— Jeremiah 9: 23-24

# Money Motivated or Prosperity Motivated?

A close friend once challenged my philosophy of life by suggesting that I was money-motivated. At first, I balked at his suggestion that making money was the force that drove me to seek success. After all, I was a Christian and a minister. Certainly money wasn't the prime motivator in my life. But after taking a hard look at my heart, I realized he was right. Growing up on the poor side of the tracks had motivated me to want to live on the prosperous side of town. In order to do that, I had to have money. By default, or by design, I became a money-driven person.

> I measured success and prosperity by one standard: how much money someone had! That's the theology of unbiblical prosperity.

I measured success and prosperity by one standard: how much money someone had! That's the theology of unbiblical prosperity.

I am glad my friend confronted me and that God taught me from His Word what real prosperity is.

# Motivation Check

*The plans of the heart belong to man, but the answer of the tongue is from the Lord. All the ways of a man are clean in his own sight, but the Lord weighs the motives. Commit your works to the Lord and your works will be established.*
— Proverbs 16:1-3

God knows our true motives. A motive is the real reason for doing the things we do. The question that we each have to answer to our satisfaction in light of God's Word is this: Am I money motivated or prosperity motivated? The way we answer will determine our life's pursuit.

Unbiblical prosperity is a popular but deceptive thief. If you are not discerning and careful, it will steal from you the possibility of attaining the balanced prosperity and success God has promised and provided for you.

## THIEF #4: Spirit of Laziness

# Laziness Produces Poverty

Someone once said God gives us the ingredients for our daily bread, but He expects us to do the baking. Only once in human history did bread fall freely from heaven for people to eat. Exodus 16:1-4 records when God graciously provided manna for Israel as they crossed the desert after the Red Sea deliverance and the triumphant exit from Egypt. Since then, man has had to work to eat.

Today there are people who do not enjoy the blessings of prosperity because they have not experienced the benefits of good, old-fashioned hard work. A thief named "Laziness" has duped them into thinking that they can get something for nothing!

Proverb 13:4 has something to say about getting something for nothing:

> *The soul of the sluggard craves and gets nothing, but the soul of the diligent is made fat.*

A sluggard is an habitually inactive, lazy person. Solomon says that the sluggard craves (yearns and has a strong desire for something), but because he is lazy, he gets nothing. Poverty is spelled L-A-Z-Y!

People who sit around waiting for their ship to come in usually find that it is a hardship. The good ship prosperity doesn't dock at the pier of the lazy person. Look up the following verses to see what the Word says about the rewards of the lazy person.

People who sit around waiting for their ship to come in usually find that it is hardship. The good ship prosperity doesn't dock at the pier of the lazy person.

| | | |
|---|---|---|
| Proverbs 18:9 | Proverbs 19:15 | Proverbs 22:15 |
| Proverbs 24:30-31 | Proverbs 26:13 | Ecclesiastes 10:18 |
| Romans 12:11 | 2 Thessalonians 3:11 | Hebrews 6:12 |

In your own words, summarize the main thought of these verses.

_____

_____

_____

_____

_____

_____

_____

The train of failure usually runs on the track of laziness!

On the other hand, the diligent soul, the person who is steady, earnest, energetic, and disciplines his desires with hard work, is the one who prospers (is made fat). Because he works hard, he receives something. Prosperity is spelled W-O-R-K!

SUMMARY

Wanting prosperity results in nothing; working for prosperity results in something.

> Wanting prosperity
> results in nothing;
> working for prosperity
> results in something.

# Work Produces Prosperity

A business manager was asked how many people worked for him. He replied, "About half of them." Sad to say, many people expect to prosper but do not want to have to work to do so. Even some Christians have bought into the "entitlement" mindset that has swept our society.

They believe life owes them whatever they want. They believe that simply because they exist they deserve benefits they didn't expend any energy or labor to get. Society exists for their benefit. They believe it is the responsibility of government, society, and others to make certain they are taken care of. They think they deserve to prosper whether they work for it or not.

Where did we ever get the idea that anyone owes us anything? That work is an unprofitable thing? This twisted, self-serving, sluggardly thinking produces lazy people who never taste the goodness of genuine prosperity.

Proverb 14:23 declares that in all labor there is profit, but mere talk leads to poverty. Note carefully what this verse declares: All labor is profitable! Some people talk about the work they are going to do; others are busy doing it. Talkers never prosper; workers do! The Bible says work is a good thing!

Study the following scriptures: Genesis 2:15, 3:19, Leviticus 23:3, Proverbs 13:11, Ecclesiastes 9:10, Ephesians 4:28, 1 Thessalonians 4:11, 2 Thessalonians 3:12. What do these verses say about work?

_____

_____

_____

_____

_____

_____

How do you feel about working?

_____

_____

_____

_____

_____

The Lord didn't burden us with work. He blessed us with it. Mankind is most positive, productive, and prosperous when working. But the devil wants you to believe that work is a bad thing. Your physical body suggests that to you, too! While some stand on the promises, others sit on the premises. It's a fact: We never stumble onto anything when we are sitting down!

Prosperity won't work if we won't! Paul bluntly told some of the Christians at Thessalonica who had become lazy, "If anyone will not work, neither let him eat" (2 Thessalonians 3:10). If you don't work, you don't eat!

> Paul bluntly told some of the Christians at Thessalonica who had become lazy, "If anyone will not work, neither let him eat" (2 Thessalonians 3:10).

## Even Ants Know How to Work!

God won't honor irresponsibility. It is irresponsible for any person to sit around and think that the Lord will provide for their needs if they won't work. According to Proverbs 6:6-11, we can learn a valuable lesson from the lowly ant:

*Go to the ant, you sluggard; consider its ways and be wise! It has no commands, no overseer or ruler, yet it stores its provisions in summer and it gathers its food at harvest. How long will you lie there, you sluggard? When will you get up from your slumber? A little sleep, a little slumber, a little folding of the hands to rest — and poverty will come on you like a bandit and scarcity like an armed man.*

## FOOD FOR THOUGHT

The dictionary is the only place you will find success before work. Everywhere else in life, work precedes success.

The spirit of laziness will do its best to rob you of the blessings derived from working to obtain prosperity.

The dictionary is the only place you will find success before work. Everywhere else in life, work precedes success.

## SELF-EVALUATION

1. Do you have a lazy bone in you? List your lazy areas.

   _____

   _____

   _____

   _____

2. Do you subscribe to the entitlement mindset in any way?

   _____

   _____

   _____

   _____

   _____

3. Do you work hard or do you hardly work?

   _____

   _____

   _____

   _____

4. How can you work on changing your lazy habits?

   _____

   _____

   _____

   _____

   _____

5. How does the work you do now contribute to your prosperity?

_____

_____

_____

_____

_____

Stop right now! Thank God for your job, your health, and the blessing of being able to work to prosper yourself.

_If you want to prosper, don't be afraid of hard work!_

## THIEF #5: Competition and Comparison

Comparison and competition are significant hurdles on the road to successful lifestyle stewardship. As twin thieves, they sneak up on us and pick our pockets before we even know what hit us. If given the opportunity, they will rob us blind and leave us empty-handed.

**First, competition and comparison distract us from God's purpose for our lives.** They entice us to take our focus off God and focus on man, instead. Our Maker has a tailor-made plan for each of us, but when we compete with, and compare ourselves to others, we begin to belittle our abilities, thinking there is nothing unique about us. We tell ourselves there are other people out in this big, wide world who are doing much better than we are. Many people appear to be much more successful than we are.

This distraction prevents us from focusing on God's personalized plan for us.

**Second, competition and comparison deceive us.** We begin to believe we have missed something. Because we aren't experiencing prosperity and success in the same way others might be, we think something must be amiss.

We think things such as: I work as hard as Mr. Jones, so why don't I get ahead like he does? Why do the Smiths have a nicer house than I do? I'm a tither, giver and servant, but my standard of living isn't like theirs. They don't give like I do, yet they seem to have more than me. I don't understand. Smith and Jones certainly resemble the "head." I look an awful lot like the tail end of life. Everyone else seems to be above me.

Competing with and comparing ourselves to others persuades us to conclude that we must be doing something wrong. We see ourselves as falling miserably

Comparison and competition are significant hurdles on the road to successful lifestyle stewardship. As twin thieves, they sneak up on us and pick our pockets before we even know what hit us. If given the opportunity, they will rob us blind and leave us empty-handed.

short of the success levels we long for, so we conclude we are obviously failing, that somehow we have missed the mark.

**Third, competition and comparison derail us.** When we remove our focus from God and His Word, we look to humanity to solve our problems. We imitate the world. We adopt its "get rich quick" schemes and "foolproof" steps to financial independence without asking any questions. We pay a heavy price for following false paths to prosperity.

By subscribing to worldly philosophies instead of God's wisdom, we cause our train to jump the track.

**Fourth, competition and comparison discourage people.** It's easy to become disheartened and discouraged when we compare our lives to others, especially when we think they are doing better than us. It's human nature to belittle ourselves when we measure our progress against others who are prospering more than we are.

Comparison and competition do have value. Healthy, properly motivated competition brings out the best in people and stretches them to maximize their potential. Comparing ourselves to others for the sake of self-improvement is commendable.

*Rather than setting our standard for prosperity according to the Bible's examples and thereby being encouraged, we mistakenly refer to men's experience, compare ourselves with their standards, compete unsuccessfully, and become discouraged.*

But there are some inherent dangers in this. Somebody is always a little bigger, stronger, prettier, thinner, faster, smarter, or richer than us. Therefore, competition and comparison can become twin killers of self-esteem. Instead of building confidence, they can crush it.

Rather than setting our standard for prosperity according to the Bible's examples and thereby being encouraged, we mistakenly refer to men's experience, compare ourselves with their standards, compete unsuccessfully, and become discouraged.

**Fifth, and finally, competition and comparison defeat us.**
We surrender to the lie that no matter how hard we may try, we won't ever prosper or succeed like others. We begin to wonder why we should pursue prosperity and seek success when other people are so far ahead of us.

Disillusioned and discouraged, we give in to pressure and give up our dreams for a prosperous life. We call it quits.

Competition and comparison are inherently unfair because:

- We are tempted to imitate others instead of being our unique selves.
- We pressure ourselves to measure success according to the world's false standards instead of the true standards found in God's Word.
- We are less likely to reach the potential God has given us to prosper according to His promises.

# How to Beat Competition and Comparison

Competition and comparison can't steal from you when you choose to adopt Paul's evaluation of God's work in his life. The great Apostle of grace made one of the most liberating statements in all of Scripture:

> *I am the least of the apostles, who am not fit to be called an apostle, because I persecuted the church of God. But by the grace of God, I am what I am, and His grace toward me did not prove vain; but I labored more than all of them, yet not I, but the grace of God with me.*
> — 1 Corinthians 15:9-10

Paul could have belittled himself by comparing himself to the other apostles in a negative way. He knew who he had been, and what he had done. Others would have put him down. But not God. Paul wrote humbly, gratefully, and triumphantly: "By the grace of God, I am what I am."

God's grace has worked in me. His marvelous, wonder-working grace has made me who I am. I am what I am and I do what I do because His grace wasn't wasted on me.

I labor hard, not to compete, but to complete what God has begun in me. By His grace, I will succeed in fulfilling God's call on my life.

Paul knew who he was. He knew who (God) and what (grace) had made him who he was, and he knew what he was to spend his life doing. He was a servant of Christ and a faithful steward of the mysteries of the Gospel (1 Corinthians 4:1-2).

Like Paul, you can:

1. Be yourself. You are special. There is nobody like you.
2. Compare yourself to Jesus. He's your standard. You don't have to be like the world because you can be like Him!

I labor hard, not to compete, but to complete what God has begun in me. By His grace, I will succeed in fulfilling God's call on my life.

3. Pursue God's prosperity plan for you! He has a success strategy specifically designed for you.

# Vision for Prosperity

*Where there is no vision, the people perish.*
— Proverbs 29:18 KJV

Vision is indispensable to success. Vision always comes before victory. To seize something, you must see it first. If you never see it, you will never be it. If you can't dream it, you will never do it. Someone once said that the poorest person is not the one who does not have a dollar, but the one who does not have a dream!

A vision is a revelation, a picture in our spirit and mind that inspires and motivates us to pursue what has been revealed to us. In Proverbs 29:18, Solomon counseled his young son that people without a vision will perish. Life without vision will not be productive, fruitful, or satisfying.

> People with no vision live unrestrained lives. Lawlessness rules. They live below the level of God's best for them. People without vision perish because they become a law unto themselves.

People with no vision live unrestrained lives. Lawlessness rules. They live below the level of God's best for them. People without vision perish because they become a law unto themselves. They don't see what good things God sees for them. They only see what they see. They pursue their will, not God's. Therefore, desires of the flesh and lustful passions control them.

Life becomes base and dull and insignificant without vision. Life without a revelation of good things becomes confusing, frustrating, and discouraging. Disappointment, failure, poverty, lack, want, and every other evil thing become the by-product of a visionless, lawless lifestyle.

On the other hand, a person with a vision will experience a fulfilling, prosperous life.

Chuck Swindoll said, "Vision is the ability to see above and beyond the majority. Vision is perception — reading the presence and power of God into one's circumstances. I sometimes think of vision as looking at life through the lens of God's eyes, seeing situations as He sees them. Too often we see things not as they are, but as we are."

Do you understand what he said? A vision is what you see through God's eyes. A vision is what God sees for you. God always sees much more and better for you than you see for yourself! To be successful and prosperous, you need to grasp God's vision for your life. You need to see for yourself what He sees for you.

You only possess what you perceive. You must look farther than your natural eyes can see. If you are not enjoying prosperity and success at this time, can you catch a vision to see beyond your current circumstances and believe God to prosper you?

Your vision is the promise of what you shall one day become.

## You Must See It Before You See It!

My wife and I enjoy landscaping our yard. Though amateurs, we have managed to put in a number of beautiful flowerbeds in the past few years. Near the entrance to our front door, we have tried numerous landscaping ideas. Shrubbery. Flowers. Shrubbery and flowers. All to no avail. Nothing we have done in that particular spot has either survived or turned out to be what we hoped it would be. Blah looking and lifeless, this strategic corner has always lacked something.

One night I walked out to the street. I often do this to view our home and yard. As I looked at the section near the entrance, I had a vision. In my imagination I saw a water pond. I envisioned white rocks lining the pool, water gently cascading down a fall. I even heard the soothing sound of the running, splashing water. I saw multi-colored petunias, pansies, and marigolds adorning it, a school of goldfish swimming freely around in it, and the Roll family enjoying their first ever water garden.

Excited, I hurried into the house to share my water pond vision with my wife. She saw the vision too — me digging the hole in the hard-as-stone clay, hauling the heavy rocks, and doing all the manual labor in hot, humid Oklahoma! We researched the project, obtained all the necessary materials, put in the pond ourselves, and guess what? We now have a beautiful little water pond, with a cascading waterfall, outside our entrance. It is exactly like what I saw.

The vision has now become reality. My dream of a soothing, restful water feature that enhanced the look and value of our front yard has come to pass.

You only possess what you perceive. You must look farther than your natural eyes can see. If you are not enjoying prosperity and success at this time, can you catch a vision to see beyond your current circumstances and believe God to prosper you?

We enjoy it, and people who walk by our home are blessed by the restful sound of rushing water!

I "saw" it before I saw it. Now I see what I saw. That's what vision is all about. If you want to be prosperous, you need a vision of prosperity.

I "saw" it before I saw it. Now I see what I saw. That's what vision is all about. If you want to be prosperous, you need a vision of prosperity.

## Prosperity Begins With Vision

Do you have a vision for prosperity and success? If you do, write your vision .

_____
_____
_____
_____
_____
_____
_____
_____
_____
_____

If you don't, read Habakkuk 2:1-3 and ask God to give you one. Then write it down.

_____
_____
_____
_____
_____
_____
_____

It's a fact of life! What you see is what you will be!

## How to Overcome Prosperity Hurdles

Having a vision for prosperity is the first step to overcoming the hurdles we have studied. The following steps will assist you in implementing the vision that you have written down. Psalm 37 details the security and prosperity of those who trust in the Lord. Study this encouraging, reassuring psalm. Then apply these simple scriptural steps to fulfilling your vision.

## See It!

Desire to prosper and succeed with all your heart. Psalm 37:4

What do you see? See yourself successful!

## Seek It!

Make a definite decision to prosper. Psalm 37:5

Commit yourself to a prosperous lifestyle.

## Seize It!

Lay hold of it in your mind, then your hand. Psalm 37:23-25

Step by step, receive what is yours.

## Secure It!

Determine to overcome all prosperity hurdles. Psalm 37:7-11

Whatever it takes, overcome every obstacle.

> Having a vision for prosperity is the first step to overcoming the hurdles we have studied.

## Sustain It!

Discipline yourself to be a successful steward. Psalm 37:3

Put in motion a lifetime plan for prosperity.

## Share It!

Delight yourself in God's blessings and dedicate yourself to sharing His blessings with others. Psalm 37:21

Give, serve people, and share with others.

## Shout It!

Give credit where credit is due. God has blessed you! Psalm 37:12-22

Glorify and praise God for prospering you!

See yourself prosperous and successful — and you will be.

# A Picture of Provision and Prosperity

*The afflicted and needy are seeking water, but there is none, and their tongue is parched with thirst; I, the Lord, will answer them Myself, as the God of Israel, I will not forsake them. I will open rivers on the bare heights, and springs in the midst of the valleys; I will make the wilderness a pool of water, and the dry land fountains of water. I will put the cedar in the wilderness, the acacia, and the myrtle, and the olive tree; I will place the juniper in the desert, together with the box tree and the cypress. That they may see and recognize, and consider and gain insight as well, that the hand of the Lord has done this, and the Holy One of Israel has created it.*
— Isaiah 41:17-20

# Lesson 7

## Faithfulness: Master Key to Successful Stewardship

*Without faith it is impossible to please Him, for he who comes to God must believe that He is, and that He is a rewarder of those who diligently seek Him.*
— Hebrews 11:6

*Let a man regard us in this manner, as servants of Christ, and stewards of the mysteries of God. In this case, moreover, it is required of stewards that one be found trustworthy (faithful).*
— 1 Corinthians 4:1-2

### PRINCIPLES
- Faith pleases God.
- Faithful people are people of faith.
- Faithfulness is required of stewards.
- Faithfulness is measured by faith and obedience.

### PURPOSE
The purpose of this lesson is to discover that faith demonstrated through faithfulness is the master key that unlocks all the doors to God's Kingdom. Faithfulness is the primary quality God looks for in the successful management of His resources. Faithfulness is evidenced by faith in and obedience to God's Word in carrying out the stewardship plan He has designed for our lives. God is looking for a lifestyle of faith, obedience, and faithfulness in His servants and stewards. Faithfulness is the master key to lifestyle stewardship.

### DISCUSSION
Like most people, I carry a key chain. House keys, automobile keys, work keys, gym locker keys, and a post office box key make up my set. I guard them very carefully and carry them on my person almost all the time. My keys are valuable pieces of metal to me because they grant me access to important places that significantly affect my lifestyle.

Just the thought of misplacing my keys, let alone actually losing them, puts my mind in a not-so-minor state of panic. Once, when I couldn't locate my key

> Faithfulness is the primary quality God looks for in the successful management of His resources. Faithfulness is evidenced by faith in and obedience to God's Word in carrying out the stewardship plan He has designed for our lives.

ring, I was panic-stricken. I began saying to myself, "Where are they? I have to find them. What will I do without them? What if somebody else gets hold of them? I can't function without them."

With every keyless moment, I became more frustrated. I also frustrated everyone else in my path. I literally turned my office, our house, and my car inside out and upside down looking for them. Guess where I found my precious keys. Right where I had last set them, of course!

Some keys are more valuable than others. They are "masters." I call them "key" keys. They give us access to important places that other keys do not. I possess a master key to my workplace. It allows me unrestricted entry through all exterior and interior doors in every building in our ministry complex. This master key gives me priority access to the management staff, support personnel, equipment, meeting rooms, products, and resources of a multi-million dollar corporation.

I can accomplish my job successfully because I possess, and have been entrusted with, a master key to all I need to be successful.

The Bible reveals that there are numerous spiritual keys to God's Kingdom. Successful stewardship requires a master key. As we learned in Lesson 3, God trusts us to manage His resources. We are His stewards. A steward is someone entrusted with another's wealth or property and charged with the responsibility of managing it in the owner's best interests. For us to succeed as stewards or managers, God entrusts us with a master key. It's faithfulness.

According to Paul in 1 Corinthians 4:2, faithfulness, or trustworthiness, is the master key to successful management of God's resources. We must be worthy of trust if we are to be fruitful stewards.

Faithfulness flows from faith. We must believe in someone (faith) if we are to manage anything for that someone (faithfulness). God's stewards put faith in Him and then faithfully manage His property for the Kingdom's benefit. Without faith we cannot be faithful, and if we are not faithful, we cannot be successful stewards.

Faithfulness is the master key in the Kingdom that grants access to fruitful, successful stewardship.

> I can accomplish my job successfully because I possess, and have been entrusted with, a master key to all I need to be successful.

# First Things First — Faith!

To have faith, or to believe, in simplest terms, means to trust. Christian faith is trusting God. biblical faith means to believe God and trust in Him. Faith is believing that He is who He says He is, and that He does what He says He will do. Christians have faith to believe that God performs what He promises (See Romans 4:17-22.).

Faith is believing without seeing. Faith is believing that which has no absolute proof. Hebrews 11:1-2 defines faith this way:

> *Faith is the assurance of things hoped for, the conviction of things not seen. For by it men of old gained approval.*

Faith is a confident trust in a deep conviction that God can be trusted. Faith is certainty that it will happen. God will do what you believe He will do! What you see first with the eye of faith will be seen with the eye of reality. Faith believes that what God says is true and that He can be trusted to do what His Word says He will do!

During the terrible days of the German blitzkrieg in World War II, a father, holding his small boy by the hand, ran from a London building that had been struck by a Nazi bomb. The front courtyard was now a crater created by the bomb. Seeking shelter as quickly as possible, the father jumped into the hole and held his arms for his son to follow.

Terrified, yet hearing his father's voice telling him to jump, the boy frantically yelled, "Father, I can't see you!"

The father, looking up at the silhouette of his son created by the burning buildings, replied, "But I can see you. Jump!"

The boy jumped because he trusted his father.

Faith means trusting our heavenly Father. Though we do not see Him, we know that He sees us. Jesus said in Mark 11:22, "Have faith in God." Putting your faith in God means you have the faith of God, the very same trust Jesus had in His Father. As Jesus had faith in His heavenly Father, so can we.

Habakkuk 2:4, Romans 1:17, and 2 Corinthians 5:7 all state that righteous men and women walk and live by faith, not by their sight. "Walking by sight" means

Faith is a confident trust in a deep conviction that God can be trusted. Faith is certainty that it will happen. God will do what you believe He will do! What you see first with the eye of faith will be seen with the eye of reality.

trusting in ourselves, our instincts, or in the opinions of others. "Walking by faith" means trusting in God and His Word.

Faith is also the biblical basis for God's approval. Faith pleases God, and He rewards faith. Read the following scriptures and answer the corresponding questions.

1.  What does Hebrews 11:2 say was the basis for the "men of old" gaining God's approval?

    _____

    _____

    _____

2.  Read Hebrews 11:6. Is it possible to please God without faith?

    _____

    _____

    _____

    _____

3.  What must a person believe if he/she is to come to know God?

    _____

    _____

    _____

    _____

4.  According to verse 6, God rewards diligent people who seek Him with what? The answer is a five letter word spelled ___ ___ ___ ___ ___ !

5.  In your own words, write what faith means to you.

    _____

    _____

    _____

    _____

    _____

    _____

    _____

Walking by faith, which is trusting God, is the scriptural secret for success in life.

> Faith is also the biblical basis for God's approval. Faith pleases God, and He rewards faith.

## SUMMARY

God's Kingdom operates according to the principle and power of faith. To receive from God, we must believe in Him. Believing in and trusting God results in receiving the blessings He has promised to the faithful. Sincere, childlike faith releases the power of heaven to meet our every need. When we speak words of faith, mountains in our lives will move. (See Mark 11:23-24.)

Faith is very personal. You cannot borrow another person's faith. You must confess your faith yourself. No one else can confess faith for you. You have to own it for it to work for you. You must put your personal faith in God if you are to see His blessing in your life. It is your responsibility and privilege to trust your heavenly Father to fulfill the promises of His Word to you.

Christian faith means trusting God to do His thing in and through you.

# Do You Need a Faith Boost?

In Romans 10:17, Paul tells us, "faith comes from hearing, and hearing by the word of Christ." As we hear and study God's Word, faith grows in our heart. The Word of God stirs up our faith in God. The Bible builds up our faith. Mature faith is God's will and goal for His followers. (See Ephesians 4:11-16.)

The following Scriptures are provided for you to study and apply to your life. These verses about faith will increase your faith and stimulate you to trust in God.

| | | |
|---|---|---|
| Proverbs 3:5-6 | Habakkuk 2:4 | Matthew 6:30 |
| Matthew 8: 10 | Matthew 9:22 | Matthew 9:29 |
| Matthew 15:28 | Matthew 17:20 | Matthew 21:21 |
| Mark 2:5 | Mark 5:34 | Mark 10:52 |
| Mark 11:22-24 | Luke 8:25 | Mark 4:35-41 |
| Luke 18:8 | Luke 18:42 | Acts 3:16 |
| Acts 6:5-8 | Acts 11:24 | Acts 14:9 |
| Acts 14:22 | Acts 15:9 | Acts 26:18 |
| Romans 1:17 | Romans 3:28 | Romans 4:5-25 |
| Romans 5:1-2 | Romans 12:3-6 | Romans 10:9-13 |
| 1 Corinthians 2:5 | 1 Corinthians 16:13 | 2 Corinthians 5:7 |
| 2 Corinthians 10:15 | 2 Corinthians 13:5 | Galatians 2:16 |
| Galatians 2:20 | Galatians 3:22-26 | Ephesians 2:8-9 |

Faith is very personal. You cannot borrow another person's faith. You must confess your faith yourself. No one else can confess faith for you. You have to own it for it to work for you. You must put your personal faith in God if you are to see His blessing in your life.

| | | |
|---|---|---|
| Ephesians 6:16 | Philippians 3:9 | 2 Thessalonians 3:1-4 |
| 2 Thessalonians 3:2 | 1 Timothy 4:6 | 1 Timothy 6:12 |
| 2 Timothy 2:22 | Hebrews 6:12 | Hebrews 11:1-2 |
| Hebrews 11:6 | Hebrews 11:39 | Hebrews 12:2 |
| James 2:5 | James 2:14-26 | James 5:15 |
| 1 Peter 1:21 | 1 Peter 5:7-9 | 2 Peter 1:5 |
| 1 John 5:4 | Jude 20 | Revelation 13:10, 14:12 |

The "Hall of Fame of Faith" is listed in Hebrews 11. Read this entire chapter, then turn to the Old Testament references where you can study in greater detail the inspiring, faith-building stories of these spiritual heroes. Learn from their examples. Apply the faith principles exercised in their lives to yours. Their faith walks will encourage you to "walk by faith."

*Faith is important because it always honors God, and God always honors faith.*

Faith is important because it always honors God, and God always honors faith.

> *An arrogant man stirs up strife, but he who trusts in the Lord will prosper. He who trusts in his own heart is a fool, but he who walks wisely will be delivered.*
> — Proverbs 28:25-26

## Obedience Is an Overflow of Faith

The first miracle Jesus performed in the New Testament is found in John 2:1-11. Jesus was attending a wedding at Cana of Galilee. His mother, Mary, and the disciples were also invited guests. At the traditional wedding reception in Jesus' day, wine was an important sign of hospitality. When the wine ran out at this reception, Mary informed Jesus and expected Him to do something about it (verse 3).

Jesus rebuked his mother, saying that His time had not yet come. According to the Lord, it was premature for Him to be revealed as miracle worker. Mary's response to her son's rebuke is contained in verse 5: His mother said to the servants, "Whatever He says to you, do it."

Mary had great insight. Much more than a mother's intuition! God's wisdom rested upon her. In her heart, she knew her son would do something about the situation. They couldn't have a marriage celebration without wine. The newlyweds and hosts would have been embarrassed. Mary knew Jesus would do something to rectify the situation.

Jesus cared about people. He cared about things like weddings, ceremonial wine, and celebrations. So Mary said to the servants on hand, "When my son does something, whatever it is, whatever He tells you to do, go ahead and do it. Obey His instructions!" She quietly, confidently ordered them to obey.

Verses 6-10 record the miracle of water turning into wine. Jesus instructed the servants to fill some water pots and take them to the head waiter. On the way, the water became wine. Excellent wine. The wine Jesus made was so good that it was called "good wine" which was ordinarily served at the beginning of the party, not the end. Jesus served them the very best.

The guests were served the very best because the servants did what Mary told them to do: "Whatever He tells you to do, do it." As servants, they were faithful to their task. They obeyed the Lord's instructions. The result? The guests drank wine and the celebration went on.

Verse 11 reveals how this miracle affected the disciples: This beginning of His signs Jesus did in Cana of Galilee, and manifested His glory, and His disciples believed in Him.

The miracle stimulated their faith. They believed in Him. From then on, they trusted Him, though not perfectly, and they began to obey His instructions. When Jesus told them to do something, (one example: sitting the great crowds down and feeding them) they did what He told them to do (Matthew 14:13-21).

Repeatedly, they proved themselves to be faithful servants and stewards because they believed in Him and they obeyed Him.

Obedience is indispensable to faithful stewardship. We can have all the faith in the world in the Lord Jesus, but if we won't take steps to obey Him, we prove ourselves unfaithful. Faithfulness is faith followed up with obedience.

## The Importance of Obedience

Obedience is so important in God's Kingdom that the prophet Samuel set King Saul straight with these hallmark words on obeying the Lord: "Has the Lord as much delight in burnt offerings and sacrifices as in obeying the voice of the Lord? Behold, to obey is better than sacrifice, and to heed than the fat of rams."

Obedience is indispensable to faithful stewardship. We can have all the faith in the world in the Lord Jesus, but if we won't take steps to obey Him, we prove ourselves unfaithful. Faithfulness is faith followed up with obedience.

Samuel told Saul that God delights in obedience. That to obey God is better than any amount of animals you may sacrifice to Him. That obedience to His Word matters more to God than anything else. Obedience is the mark of faithful servants and stewards of the living God. Stop relying on sacrifices and start obeying.

The Word of God says these things about obedience in the life of the believer:
- Obedience must be whole-hearted.                              Deut. 26:16
- Obedience is the price of success.                              Joshua 1:8
- Obedience secures entrance into God's Kingdom.                 Matthew 7:21
- Obedience is the foundational rock of godly character.         Matthew 7:24
- Obedience is essential to membership in God's family.          Matthew 12:50
- Obedience is the key to spiritual knowledge.                   John 7:17
- Obedience secures the blessing of divine fellowship.           John 14:23
- Obedience is our duty.                                         Acts 5:29

Christ is our supreme example of obedience that flowed from faith. See John 14:31, John 15:10, Romans 5:19, Hebrews 5:8, and 10:9. Jesus always did whatever God told Him to do! The Son of God proved Himself faithful by doing whatever the Father told Him to do.

> Christ is our supreme example of obedience that flowed from faith.

What blessings of obedience are found in Exodus 19:5, Deuteronomy 4:30, 5:29, 7:12, 28:1, 1 Kings 3:14, Job 36:11, Zechariah 3:7, James 1:25, 1 John 3:22, and Revelation 22:14?

_____

_____

_____

_____

_____

_____

_____

_____

These blessings belong to faithful servants and stewards of the Lord.

# Do What He Tells You to Do!

Below are five simple signs of obedience of every faithful steward.

1.  **Do whatever He tells you to do!**
    If God tells you to visit a shut-in, write an offering check, mow someone's grass, send a missionary a care package, or teach a Sunday school class — whatever it is, do it! Obey His assignment.

2.  **Do it with what He tells you!**
    Take the exact amount of money, contact the specific persons, assemble the materials, or make the phone call. Do whatever He tells you to do with exactly what He tells you!

3.  **Do it when He tells you!**
    If He says this minute, next week, next month, this afternoon, or the beginning of next year. Do it then! Not a minute earlier or later. Do it when He says you re supposed to.

4.  **Do it the way He tells you!**
    Whatever the process, the people, plans, products, resources, networking, connections, or contacts. Obey His explicit instructions to the last detail!

5.  **Do it for the purpose (why) He tells you!**
    Do whatever He asks for the express reason He asks you. No other purpose but the one He revealed to you when He gave you this task.

## An Inspiring Example of Obedience

Read the story of Elijah and the woman of Zarephath found in 1 Kings 17. Write your observations concerning how each took the five steps of obedience outlined above. Be very specific. Qualify your findings by noting the verse where you observed the obedience principle.

|  | ELIJAH | VERSE |
|---|---|---|
| 1. | _____ | _____ |
| 2. | _____ | _____ |
| 3. | _____ | _____ |
| 4. | _____ | _____ |
| 5. | _____ | _____ |

How did God bless Elijah's obedience in this miraculous story?

WOMAN OF ZAREPATH                    VERSE

1._____          _____

2._____          _____

3._____          _____

4._____          _____

5._____          _____

In what ways did God bless the woman's obedience in this incident?

_____

_____

_____

_____

_____

What principles of obedience did you learn from this story?

_____

_____

_____

_____

_____

What do Mary's words in John 2:5 mean to you in your everyday life?

Faithful people have
faith in and are obedient
to God.

_____

_____

_____

_____

_____

The bottom line is this: Faithful stewards do whatever God tells them to do!

## Faith Plus Obedience Equals Faithfulness

Faithful people have faith in and are obedient to God. According to the dictionary, to be faithful means "to be steadfast in your affection or allegiance, loyal, firm in adherence to promises or in observance of duty; conscientious, binding, constant, given with strong assurance."

This describes God perfectly! Lamentations 3:22-23 says of God:

*The Lord's lovingkindnesses indeed never cease, for His compassions never fail, they are new every morning; great is thy faithfulness.*

Faithfulness is one of Almighty God's greatest attributes. God is steadfast in His love and care for us. He never wavers in His allegiance to us. His unconditional love is binding. It's ours, all the time. Nothing can separate us from His love (Romans 8:31-39). We can depend on our Heavenly Father to love us even when we don't love ourselves. His affection for His children is constant. He is loyal in His love.

God makes magnificent promises in His Word. He faithfully performs what He promises. He is faithful to keep His Word. He commits Himself to keep His promises. He never breaks those promises. God is the ultimate promise keeper!

God keeps His covenant with His children. His agreement with us is an everlasting covenant (Genesis 17:7). In faithfulness, He has committed Himself to keep His covenant for all generations who believe in Him. Men may become unfaithful and let you down. God never will!

> As a Christian, you can count on God. He is The Faithful One! He is who He says He is. He does what He says He will do! He can be trusted!

As a Christian, you can count on God. He is the Faithful One! He is who He says He is and He does what He says He will do! He can be trusted! He will always come through for you because He cannot be unfaithful.

God is faithful. He calls us to be His faithful stewards. His example inspires us to be faithful in our assignment as managers of His resources.

There is no question that we can count on God. The real question is: Can God count on us to be faithful?

# Three Key Characteristics of a Faithful Steward

*It is required of stewards that one be found trustworthy (faithful)*
— 1 Corinthians 4:2

Faithful. Trustworthy. Two of Paul's favorite words when writing in the New Testament. He used faithfulness to describe key figures in the biblical history. The fathers/pillars of Christianity were all faithful in their lives and ministries.

| | | |
|---|---|---|
| Abraham | Faithful Abraham | Galatians 3:9 |
| Moses | Moses was faithful in his house | Hebrews 3: 2,5 |
| Jesus Christ | He was faithful to Him who appointed Him | Hebrews 3:2 |
| Paul himself | He (God) counted me faithful | 1 Timothy 1:12 |

Paul also used the word *faithful* in describing his trustworthy ministry partners.

| | |
|---|---|
| Colossians 1:2 | to the saints and faithful brethren in Christ at Colossae |
| Colossians 1:7 | Epaphras, a faithful servant of Christ on our behalf |
| Colossians 4:7 | Tychius, our beloved brother and faithful servant |
| 1 Peter 5:12 | Silvanus, our faithful brother |
| Colossians 4:9 | Onesimus, our faithful and beloved brother |
| 1 Corinthians 4:7 | Timothy, my beloved son and faithful child in the Lord |

These were very special people, singled out because they were different from the crowd. Paul loved them and believed in them. The reason? Paul found each of them worthy of trust. He could count on them to be faithful to their assigned tasks. They had established a personal track record of faithfulness as servants and stewards of Christ.

The Apostle Paul was Timothy's spiritual father and ministry mentor. In 1 Timothy 6:20-21,the conclusion of Paul's letter to his son in the faith, Paul exhorted Timothy to be careful to keep what God had entrusted to him.

> *O, Timothy, guard (keep faithfully) what has been entrusted to you, avoiding worldly and empty chatter and the opposing arguments of what is falsely called knowledge — which some have professed and thus have gone astray from the faith. Grace be with you.*

Keep God's Word in your heart. Refuse the empty chatter and arguments of this world. Stay on course by guarding what God has entrusted to you. Be found faithful in all you do as His representative.

In the busyness of life and ministry, Timothy, never forget to faithfully guard what God has entrusted to your care. Be diligent and faithful to be a trusted and worthy servant and steward of Christ. Live a life of faithful stewardship that pleases God and brings good to people. I have trained you in the faith. Keep God's Word in your heart. Refuse the empty chatter and arguments of this world. Stay on course by guarding what God has entrusted to you. Be found faithful in all you do as His representative.

All the previously mentioned faithful servants of Christ, including Timothy, possessed common characteristics that set them apart as trustworthy stewards. Next, we'll look at the three characteristics which distinguish these trusted servants of the Lord. Without these three key characteristics, faithful stewardship is not possible.

# Lessons From an Unrighteous Steward:
## Luke 16:1-13

Jesus told His disciples a story about a rich man who had a steward who was squandering his master's possessions (v. 1). The master required the steward to give an account of his stewardship. The wealthy man was so upset with the unfaithful steward that he told him he could no longer manage his possessions and property (v. 2).

The steward didn't like the fact that he was being removed from management. He would no longer hold a job, so he thought about his future. Verses 3-7 tell us he devised a plan. He had his master's debtors adjust, hoping that when the master let him go, those people would appreciate the fact that he had reduced their debts, and would receive him when he was unemployed. The master praised the unrighteous steward's shrewdness.

Verse 9 records the verdict of the unrighteous steward. If we make unrighteous mammon (money) our friend, it will fail us. So, we had better be good managers of the totality of life if we are not to perish, but be received into eternity.

Immediately after telling this revealing parable, Jesus taught His followers three key characteristics of faithful stewards.

## 1. Faithful Stewards Are Faithful in Little Things

> *He who is faithful in a very little thing is faithful also in much; and he who is unrighteous in a very little thing is unrighteous in much.*
> — Luke 16:10

Growing up I was tempted to think that if I just had more things, bigger things, newer things, or better things that I would take good care of them. I am glad I had a wise, sensible mother who taught me the principle of taking good care of what you have. She showed me the value of being faithful to keep an old house clean, deliver a newspaper properly to one subscriber as well as a hundred, enjoy a picnic lunch and playground time at the park as much as a day at Disneyland, and so forth. Though my mom didn't teach me specifically from the scriptures, she knew from experience that faithfulness in little things would lead to faithfulness in big things.

Jesus said, "He who is faithful in a very little thing..." A very little thing. Life is made up of little things. Big things are the sum total of a lot of little

If we make unrighteous mammon (money) our friend, it will fail us. Therefore, we had better be good managers of the totality of life if we are not to perish, but be received into eternity.

things along the way. Our faithfulness is tested in the little events of life. Small assignments. Tiny tasks. If you can't be trusted with a little, you won't faithfully handle a lot.

If you aren't faithful to prepare properly to preach to a crowd of fifty, you won't be trusted to preach to a congregation of five hundred or five thousand. If you aren't trustworthy working for minimum wage at McDonald's, you won't be faithful working for big bucks at a major corporation. If you can't be trusted to write a tithe check from twenty dollars, you won't write one from two hundred, two thousand, or twenty thousand dollars, either. If you aren't faithful to change the oil in your old car, keep it clean and in good running order, God won't trust you with a new, more expensive automobile. It's that simple.

In the parable of the talents, Matthew 25:14-30, two servants were rewarded and one was not. The successful stewards (See verses 20-23.) were praised — well done, good and faithful servant, and were put in charge of much more than they had previously managed and could ever dream of because they were faithful with a few things.

Faithful with a few things. Trustworthiness is proven in the little things. The jobs nobody else wants. Tasks with no headlines. The lowly, menial assignments behind the scenes. Doing things that others think are beneath their position and dignity.

Whether men notice or not, Jesus sees how we handle the undesirable, unnoticed, insignificant little things in life. It's not the amount or size of the assignment. It's the attitude. Faithful stewards are faithful whether the task is great or small. They position themselves for management of greater tasks because they prove themselves trustworthy in the smaller ones.

Many Christians don't get to experience the enjoyment of big things because they can't be trusted with them. They wonder why they don't get the break of a big job and salary; why they don't have a large ministry; why they don't have nice things to enjoy. It's simple. God can't trust them with more. They didn't handle the little things properly, so why should He trust them with bigger things? He doesn't, and He won't.

Unfaithfulness in "a very little thing" is proof you won't be faithful in a very big thing. Faithfulness in "a very little thing" is evidence of an attitude of trustworthiness that qualifies you for a promotion to management of much bigger things.

If you aren't trustworthy working for minimum wage at McDonald's, you won't be faithful working for big bucks at a major corporation. If you can't be trusted to write a tithe check from twenty dollars, you won't write one from two hundred, two thousand, or twenty thousand dollars, either.

## SELF-EVALUATION

Are you faithful with the small assignments God gives you?

_____

_____

_____

List a recent "little thing" you were asked to do. How did you handle it?

_____

_____

_____

_____

_____

Can God truly trust you with the little things of life?

_____

_____

_____

Unfaithfulness in "a very little thing" is proof you won't be faithful in a very big thing. Faithfulness in "a very little thing" is evidence of an attitude of trustworthiness that qualifies you for a promotion to management of much bigger things.

Based on your attitude and behavior in handling little things, are you qualified for bigger things from God?

_____

_____

_____

If you are looking forward to bigger things in the future, what do you need to do to adjust your attitude today towards managing the little things the Lord sends your way?

_____

_____

_____

## REMEMBER
Faithful in little means faithful in much!

## 2. Faithful Stewards Are Faithful in Managing Money

_If therefore you have not been faithful in the use of unrighteous mammon, who will entrust the true riches to you?_
— Luke 16:11

Mammon is another word for money. Jesus makes a profound statement regarding the management of money. First, the Lord calls money unrighteous. Money and material riches are not holy, pure, and sacred in the sight of God. The use of money is very important, but money itself is not, even though we think it is. He also implies in this verse that "unrighteous mammon" does not qualify as the true riches in life. There are obviously some things much more important than mere dollars and cents! In the larger scheme of things, money ranks pretty low on the list of what really counts.

In Matthew 6:24 Jesus says, "No one can serve two masters; for either he will hate the one and love the other, or he will hold to one and despise the other. You cannot serve God and mammon (money)." You can only have one master. That's the way our Creator wired you. It is not possible to serve God and money at the same time. You must be mastered by one and you must master the other. You have the freedom to choose who you will serve, God or money. God's choice for you is to serve Him and for money to serve you.

> If first, you serve the Lord, and second, you manage money well, then you will receive from God the real riches in life. But note: If you are not faithful to manage money well, you will never be entrusted with true riches.

If first, you serve the Lord, and second, you manage money well, then you will receive from God the real riches in life. But note: If you are not faithful to manage money well, you will never be entrusted with true riches. Faithful management of money is a test of trustworthiness — more of a test than many people know.

Many people are found unfaithful as stewards because they fail to manage their money well. If a person can't manage a little money, be certain, God won't trust them with a lot!

It is imperative that you understand that for all trustworthy stewards, managing money faithfully is a biblical prerequisite to managing the really important things and resources life has to offer. How you handle your money is a significant indicator of how you would handle really valuable things.

## SELF-EVALUATION
When the truth is told concerning serving God or money, who is your real Master?

_____

_____

_____

_____

Does your lifestyle demonstrate that God is your master and money is your servant? Support your position.

_____

_____

_____

_____

_____

Do you trust yourself with money? Do other people trust you with money (yours or theirs)? Can God trust you with money? Small amounts? Large amounts?

_____

_____

_____

_____

What are the "true riches" in life?

_____

_____

_____

_____

## REMEMBER
If you want to be trusted with true riches, faithfully manage your money.

## 3. Faithful Stewards Are Faithful With Other People's Things

*If you have not been faithful in the use of that which is another's, who will give you that which is your own?*
— Luke 16:12

The parables that we have studied all have to do with a servant managing someone else's possessions or property. In the verse above, Jesus sends a clear message: If you aren't faithful with other people's possessions, God won't give you opportunity to be unfaithful with your own! You must be found faithful in managing another man's things before you will be trusted with your own things to manage.

In the early years of our marriage, my wife and I rented apartments, duplexes and small houses that were owned by other people. From the day we moved in to the day we moved out, we were very faithful to take excellent care of other people's property. It was our practice to leave each place in better condition than we found it, without exception. I believe that is why today we have been blessed with our own home.

Everybody wants to own something and do their own thing. That's fine. But the road to your own things runs right through other people's things. Faithful stewards manage other people's things well.

## SELF-EVALUATION

If you want to own your own business someday, are you faithful in your service to another businessperson who employs you? Do you treat his buildings, vehicles, computers, office space, and staff as if they were your own?

If you want to be a homeowner in the future, do you take good care of your landlord's apartment or house? Do you keep it up as though you own it? Does your rental property not look different from the typical rental units?

Would your employer, landlord, or pastor say that you have been faithful in that which belongs to another person?

Remember, if you want to have your own possessions and property to manage, first be faithful in managing another person's property and possessions.

> *The Lord will repay each man for his righteousness and faithfulness.*
> — 1 Samuel 26:23

> Everybody wants to own something and do their own thing. That's fine. But the road to your own things runs right through other people's things. Faithful stewards manage other people's things well.

# Lesson 8

## Stewards As Givers

*Give, and it will be given unto you; good measure, pressed down, shaken together, running over, they will pour into your lap. For by your standard of measure it will be measured to you in return.*
— Luke 6:38

*I testify that according to their ability, and beyond their ability they gave of their own accord, begging us with much entreaty for the favor of participation in the support of the saints, and this, not as we had expected, but they first gave themselves to the Lord and to us by the will of God.*
— 2 Corinthians 8:3-5

### PRINCIPLES
- Giving is the joy of living.
- In God's Kingdom, we receive in proportion to what we give.
- Giving is a way of living for successful stewards.

### PURPOSE
Our primary objective in this chapter is to learn that giving is the way to blessing in the Kingdom of God. Giving is a high and holy hallmark of servants and stewards of Christ. Good stewards are good givers. They are people who have come to know the power, blessing, and joy of being a giver.

What we receive in life is largely determined by what we give in life. Faithful managers of God's resources practice giving as a way of life. Good stewards live to give. We will discover from our study that God is the greatest giver; God's people are called to be givers after Christ's example, and God richly rewards and blesses generous givers.

### DISCUSSION
Billy Graham has said, "God has given us two hands — one for receiving and the other for giving." Having been raised in a family where prosperity was unknown, I learned to focus on the receiving hand. Because we had little, my hand was usually out to receive. Don't misunderstand. Our household did do some giving. We certainly were not raised to be only takers. We were given some basic instruction about the value and importance of giving. But, in all honesty, there wasn't a whole lot to give in those days!

> Giving is a high and holy hallmark of servants and stewards of Christ. Good stewards are good givers. They are people who have come to know the power, blessing, and joy of being a giver.

Out of necessity, and probably by default, I developed a life philosophy that centered on what I could receive, not what I could give. Life was a contest to see how much you could get.

After I accepted Christ, God's Word began to change my thinking. As I studied the Bible, the subject of giving seemed to pop up on nearly every page. I began to realize that giving is a major theme that is woven throughout the fabric of God's Word. Paul amplified this truth for me when he said in Acts 20:35, "In everything I showed you that by working hard in this manner you must help the weak and remember the words of the Lord Jesus, that He Himself said, "It is more blessed to give than to receive."

> The Lord Jesus Himself told His followers that giving and receiving were part of life and that giving superseded receiving in blessing.

The Lord Jesus Himself told His followers that giving and receiving were part of life and that giving superseded receiving in blessing. Jesus put His personal seal of approval on giving. This verse doesn't say that receiving is not blessed. It is. But more (greater or increased) blessing comes through giving. We are extra-blessed and God is well pleased when we give.

If it is more blessed to give than receive, and it is, then it stands to reason that we should spend more of our time and energy giving than receiving.

# Giving and Stewardship

Matthew 5, 6, and 7 contain what the Bible calls the Beatitudes. In these passages of scripture, Jesus taught Kingdom principles, attitudes, and actions that set the lifestyle of a Christian apart from the non-Christian. Robert Schuller remarked in a sermon "The Beatitudes are the BE-attitudes." What Christians should believe and how they should behave form the essence of the Beatitudes.

Giving is central to the concept of biblical stewardship. In Matthew 5:42, the Lord said, "Give to him who asks of you, and do not turn away from him who wants to borrow from you." Jesus tells us to be ready to give. If someone asks for assistance, and you have the ability to help, do it. Giving is very important in the life of a consecrated believer. Giving is a BE-attitude!

## SOMETHING TO THINK ABOUT

There can be no faithful management of God's resources unless we give. Stewards receive resources from God. Through faithful management of their God-given resources, they bless others by sharing what they have. Sharing comes by giving. Giving and stewardship cannot be divorced from one another. They go hand in hand.

A Christian's greatness is measured by his giving as well as his service. The Bible's bottom line concerning greatness in the Kingdom is serving and giving.

Read Matthew 20:26-28, and answer the following questions.

1.  If you want to be great, what must you do? (v. 26).

    _____

    _____

    _____

    _____

2.  If you want to finish first in life, what is required? (v. 27).

    _____

    _____

    _____

    _____

    It's a fact: What we receive is greatly determined by what we give.

3.  Christians are to be Christ-like. The word *Christian* literally means to be "a little Christ." According to verse 28, what two things must a believer do to be like Jesus? _____ and _____.

Successful stewardship demands that we practice giving as part of our daily life. God's Word also promises that blessing and prosperity come to those who give.

# Give, and Others Will Give to You!

Life for some people is like standing in front of a wood burning fireplace, not putting any wood in, yet saying, "Give me some heat." We know from experience there can be no heat without wood. If we want heat, we must chop some wood and put it on the fire. If we want something from life, we must give something to life. There is no something for nothing. It's a fact: What we receive is greatly determined by what we give.

Let's look at a great "something for something" scripture. Read Luke 6:38 several times. Meditate upon it. Then write in your own words what this scripture means to you.

_____

_____

_____

_____

_____

_____

"Give, and it will be given to you." These eight words form a spiritual principle that touches our lives in a very profound way. These eight great words on giving reveal a spiritual law that can literally change your world. It is called the law of reciprocity.

The word *reciprocate* means "to give and take mutually, to return in kind or degree, to make a return for something." Reciprocity involves a relationship between at least two parties. When people reciprocate, they return to the other person something similar to what he has received. For example, if you smile at someone, they will most likely reciprocate — smile back. If you strike someone, chances are they will hit you back. If you express kindness, you are almost certain to have someone express kindness in return. If you are critical of everything and everyone, you can expect to receive critical judgment from others. If you do a good deed for another, the law of reciprocity says they will return a good deed to you.

The Bible discusses the law of reciprocity: "Give, and it will be given to you." Jesus understood the idea of something for something. He said that if we give, people will reciprocate, give back to us.

Luke 6:38 can be broken into four important concepts. All four of these concepts must be in play for the law of reciprocity to work.

## 1. First, You Must Give

Your part in this give/receive formula is to give. The law of reciprocity can't function unless someone first gives something. You must give to get. No giving, no receiving! Give. One simple, active verb. Your part and responsibility is to give. Your act of giving sets off the reaction of God and others. Reciprocal blessing always begins with give.

## 2. You Give, Then You Receive

Please note the promise here. "Give, and it will be given to you." This verse does not say that if you give, maybe someone will give to you, or if you're lucky, you might receive something from others. Not "maybe" or "might" but "will." The Word couldn't be clearer. Give, and you can count on being given to! This verse shows us a give-give promise. God Himself stands behind the giver with a guarantee of receiving. When we give, God makes sure that what we need will be given to us.

Give-give is a win-win proposition. You win by giving, and you win by receiving. Others gain when you give to them; you gain when they give to you. Everybody wins when everybody gives! If people want to really start living, they need to start giving!

## 3. You Give, Then You Receive from Other People

Note that the "it" in "it will" is given by the "they" in "they will pour," which refers to people. God gives through people. You give, and God gives back to you through other people. Too many people think that when they give only God can give back to them. They miss the fact that God's giving to us most often comes in one form or another through human means. God can certainly give without the assistance of people. He has before. But His preferred method of giving is to use people as channels of His blessing.

When we give, people will give to us. Look how they reciprocate: "good measure, pressed down, shaken together, running over, they will pour into your lap." What a wonderful picture of prosperity and abundance!

The word *lap* or *bosom* in the KING JAMES VERSION refers to a fold or pocket in a Jewish person's outer garment. This pocket hung over a girdle that was worn underneath. People would pass each other and deposit money, blessings, business papers, inheritance items, and other means of material wealth into these pockets. The picture here is that of a pocket so full that it overflows and spills out on the ground.

Another biblical picture here is that of a large measure of grain being harvested, sifted, and then stored in a container. The grain is packed in the container. More and more grain is shaken together and pressed down until the container finally overflows. The abundance of grain spills over the top, overflowing into the farmer's lap.

When you pour it out through giving, God pours it on through giving back to you.

When we give, people will give to us. Look how they reciprocate: "good measure, pressed down, shaken together, running over, they will pour into your lap." What a wonderful picture of prosperity and abundance!

### 4. You Give, Then You Receive from People According to What You Have Given

People reap what they sow. The law of sowing and reaping is found in Galatians 6:7-8. Second Corinthians 9:6 teaches us that how much we reap is determined by how much we sow. Whatever measure, or standard of giving we use, that is what we receive.

> *This I say, he who sows sparingly, shall also reap sparingly; and he who sows bountifully, shall also reap bountifully.*
> — Galatians 6:7-8

Paul's inspired instruction is clear: You get according to what you give. If you give a little, you receive a little. If you give a lot, you receive a lot.

It stands to reason that if you want to receive more, you must give more. To give "bountifully" requires that you understand biblical principles concerning bountiful, or generous giving. The first truth you need to grasp if you are to become a good giver is that God Himself is your example for giving.

## God, the Greatest Giver

Good stewards of Jesus Christ don't have to be hit over the head to give. Principles, not plaster, motivate them to give. They know from the Bible that Christianity is all about giving.

There's a story told about a church that was raising funds to repair the ceiling. During a business meeting, the minister was calling upon members for their financial pledges. One of the leaders of the church rose from his seat and said, "I pledge five dollars." At that moment, a piece of plaster fell on his head. Half-stunned, he mumbled, "Fifty dollars". Immediately, the pastor prayed, "Oh Lord, hit him again!"

Good stewards of Jesus Christ don't have to be hit over the head to give. Principles, not plaster, motivate them to give. They know from the Bible that Christianity is all about giving. The scriptural tone and tenor for Christians becoming givers is found in the most well-known and beloved verse in the Bible:

> *God so loved the world that He gave His only begotten Son, that whoever believes in Him, should not perish, but have eternal life.*
> — John 3:16

When we study how God gives to us, we find that He gives to us lovingly, graciously, and generously.

## 1. Lovingly

Based on John 3:16, God gives because He loves! God is the first and greatest giver. The Gospel (Good news) is all about a wonderful gift God has given to us. This verse among verses announces that God loved fallen man so much that He gave His only Son. Because God loved, He gave. Love moved God to give. His unselfish, sacrificial giving provided the way for sinners to receive forgiveness of sin and the gift of eternal life through faith in Jesus Christ. (See Romans 3:23, 5:8, 6:23.)

Salvation is the gift of gifts! Not only did God secure salvation for us through the giving of His Son, Romans 8:32 declares that through Jesus, God also freely gives us all things.

> *He who did not spare His own Son, but delivered Him up for us all, how will He not also with him freely give us all things?*
> — Romans 8:32

Look up the following verses and think about some of the "things" God has given you.

| | |
|---|---|
| Life and breath | Isaiah 42:5 |
| Food, clothing, shelter | Matthew 6:25-33 |
| Protection and security | Psalm 62 |
| Peace | 2 Thessalonians 3:16 |
| Deliverance | Isaiah 41:10 |
| Strength and power | Psalm 68:35 |
| Family and children | Psalm 127:3 |
| New hearts | Ezekiel 11:19 |
| Faith | Ephesians 2:8-9 |
| Word of God | 2 Timothy 3:16 |
| Victory | Revelation 20-22 |

Salvation is the gift of gifts! Not only did God secure salvation for us through the giving of His Son, Romans 8:32 declares that through Jesus, God also freely gives us all things.

What are some other things that you value that you can add to this list?

_____

_____

_____

_____

_____

## 2. Graciously

Grace refers to the unmerited favor of God. Though we do not deserve His gifts, He chooses out of His heart of love, mercy, and grace to bless us.

Matthew 5:45 makes a statement about grace: "For He causes His sun to rise on the evil and on the good, and sends rain on the righteous and the unrighteous. According to this verse, our Maker blesses us whether we deserve it or not. God Gives Because He Is Good and Gracious!

## 3. Generously

The God of the Bible is generous, never greedy or stingy. Paul had something to say about God's generosity in the following scriptures.

*Unto Him who is able to do exceeding abundantly beyond all that we ask or think, according to the power that works within us*
— Ephesians 3:20

*God is able to make all grace abound to you, that always having all sufficiency in everything, you may have an abundance for every good deed.*
— 2 Corinthians 9:8

Make no mistake about it, God is generous with His gifts!

Take a look at your life. God has given you many wonderful gifts. What a great giver He is! In Him and through Him you have more than enough. Pause for a moment and praise God for the gifts He has given you.

## SUMMARY

God is a great giver Who gives good gifts to His children. Everything you need to succeed in life is given to you at no charge. God's children are required to be faithful managers of these free gifts. Your privilege and responsibility is to enjoy God's gracious gifts and share what you have received with others.

You can be a good giver because God Himself has shown you how to give.

# God's People as Givers

It's a biblical truth that God uses people to help people. Study the following Scriptures in their context. These exhortations concerning giving and the examples of people of God who gave to others will inspire you to do the same.

> God is a great giver Who gives good gifts to His children. Everything you need to succeed in life is given to you at no charge

Deuteronomy 15:12-14, Proverbs 25:21, Ecclesiastes 11:1, Isaiah 58:7, Matthew 5:42, Matthew 19:21, Luke 12:33, Ruth 2:15, 2 Kings 6:22, 2 Chronicles 28:15, Isaiah 21:14, and Luke 10:34-35.

The New Testament church was a giving church. Let's take a detailed look at a specific instance to see the church giving according to the example Jesus set.

A healing miracle took place in Acts 3:1-10. This was the first incidence the church had opportunity to give after the infilling of the Holy Spirit at Pentecost.

A healing miracle took place in Acts 3:1-10. This was the first incidence after the infilling of the Holy Spirit at Pentecost where the church had opportunity to give.

## Setting (vv. 1-2)

Peter and John went to the temple to pray, a normal activity for them, part of their Christian lifestyle. A man who had never walked (over forty years old and lame from birth, according to Acts 4:22) was sitting near the Temple entrance begging for money. The lame man was there every day.

## Situation (v. 3)

The lame man saw Peter and John and asked them for financial assistance.

## Ministry Opportunity (v. 4)

Peter and John do not ignore the man. They give him their attention. Peter and John ask the lame beggar to focus his attention on them.

## What Was Given (vv. 5-6)

The lame man expected to receive something. Peter looked him right in the eye and boldly declared: "I do not possess silver and gold, but what I do have, I give to you; in the name of Jesus Christ the Nazarene — walk! Peter didn't have any money at that time, but he did have faith in Jesus. Peter gave what he had — an invitation for the man to experience a miracle, to rise and walk in Jesus' name.

## Ministry Result (vv. 7-10)

Peter reached out to touch the man with his hand. As he raised him up, the man's ankles and feet were "immediately" strengthened. The lame man now was standing, walking, leaping, and praising God. Rejoicing in his ability to walk, he ran into the Temple to give witness of his miracle. The people took note of him, marveled at his healing, and were filled with wonder and amazement at what they had just witnessed with their own eyes. God was glorified!

## Principle: Give What You Have to Give

This lame man didn't need a handout. He needed a hand up! He needed a miracle more than he needed money! Peter didn't hesitate to give the man what he had.

He gave the man his time and attention, his compassion and personal assistance, and he ministered his spiritual gifts of faith and the working of miracles.

Walking by faith as a servant of Christ and a good steward of the Gospel, Peter gave this man what he needed most — an opportunity for a miracle. Peter's faith in Jesus stirred up the beggar's faith for himself to be healed in the name of Jesus.

If Peter had not given what he had, the man would have remained a lame beggar. The lame were healed during Jesus' ministry because Jesus gave. Because Peter was a giver, a hopelessly needy man went from lame to leaping, paralysis to praise, sadness to gladness! As a giving man, Peter followed in the footsteps of His Lord and Savior.

God was glorified and men were edified because Peter gave!

## Application

God calls us, as stewards of His gifts, to give what we have. The Lord never asks His people to give what they don't have. Second Corinthians 8:12 says if the readiness is present, it is acceptable according to what a man has, not according to what he does not have. The devil will trick people out of giving by convincing them that they can't give because they don't have anything to give. That's utter nonsense. A lie.

Everyone has something to give.
- A destitute widow gave her only jar of oil and God multiplied it until its value paid her debt and provided income for her and her sons (2 Kings 4:1-7).
- A boy gladly gave up his sack lunch of bread and fish that God used to feed 5,000 men and their families who were hungry (Matthew 14:23-31).
- A poor woman put her last pennies into the Temple offering and because Jesus remarked how great her gift was, she is remembered in God's Word for all time (Luke 21:1-4).
- A worshipper poured out expensive perfume to honor the Lord as He prepared for His upcoming death and resurrection. Jesus used her example to teach about what is and what is not important in life. (John 12:1-8).
- A former tax collector opened his home to Jesus. The lives of Zaccheus, his family, and others were changed forever because he gave hospitality (Luke 19:1-10).

Everyone, including you, has something to give in Jesus' name.

> God calls us, as stewards of His gifts, to give what we have. The Lord never asks His people to give what they don't have.

> Everyone, including you, has something to give in Jesus' name.

## FURTHER STUDY

We witness the church in 2 Corinthians 8:1-14 giving financial assistance to other Christians who were experiencing a season of difficulty.

1. What had been given to the Macedonian churches? (v. 1)

   _____

   _____

   _____

2. Note carefully the circumstances of the Macedonian churches. It was a time of great affliction and deep poverty in their own lives. Yet while they were in need, they gave to others in need. According to verse 2, with what kind of attitude did they give?

   _____

   _____

   _____

3. Name the three ways Paul says this church gave (v. 3).

   _____

   _____

   _____

   _____

   _____

4. In verse 4, what did the Macedonians "beg" Paul that they might do?

   _____

   _____

   _____

5. The Macedonians' joyful, sacrificial giving happened because they first gave themselves to whom? (v. 5).

   _____

   _____

   _____

   _____

6. Write in your own words what you think about the Macedonian givers.

   _____

   _____

   _____

SUMMARY

The Macedonian Christians were great givers. They gave themselves to the Lord, then they gave themselves and their gifts to men. They gave willingly, according to their ability and even beyond their ability. With joy and a desire to be helpful, they asked if they could participate in giving. Their generous giving resulted in lightening the load of the Christians in Jerusalem who had fallen on hard times.

# Give Like Your Heavenly Daddy Gives

> The Macedonian Christians were great givers. They gave themselves to the Lord, then they gave themselves and their gifts to men.

At the conclusion of a worship service, a little boy hurried to the foyer to find an usher. He pulled a tarnished penny from his trouser pocket and placed it in the offering plate. Upon returning to his mother, he announced what he had done. Curiosity got the best of mom. She asked her son why he put his penny in the plate. He promptly replied, "I saw daddy give his money to God, and I want to be just like my daddy." If you want to be like your Father in heaven, be a giver.

## PERSONAL APPLICATION

Keeping in mind the two principles "give what you have" from Acts 3:1-10 and "give according to your ability" from 2 Corinthians 8:1-5, respond to the following.

1. What do you have to give? Make a thorough list of your talents, gifts, material resources, etc.

   _____

   _____

   _____

   _____

   _____

2. Are you giving what you have?

   _____

3. Is your level of giving according to your true ability?

   _____

4. Are you giving even beyond your ability?

   _____

5.  I will take these specific steps to become a better steward in the area of giving.

1-_____

2-_____

3-_____

4-_____

5-_____

*Heal the sick, raise the dead, cleanse the lepers, cast out demons; freely you received, freely give.*
— Matthew 10:8

# Be Generous With God's Gifts

Very early in my Christian life, the Lord placed me under the leadership of a very godly and generous man. Twenty-five years later, I am so grateful to God for allowing me to witness firsthand Christian generosity in action. I am forever indebted to this pastor. His generous lifestyle forever changed my attitude toward giving. I caught the joy and blessings of being a generous giver. That was a radical change for me.

Before my conversion, most of my experience with giving was limited to observing people who lived on the selfish, greedy, and stingy side of life. Their hands were closed to the needs of others. Giving the least, not the most, was their motto.

Generous people are liberal when it comes to giving. Their hands are open, not closed. How much they can give, not how little, is their creed. A person with a generous spirit is gracious, magnanimous, and looks at life through the eyes of abundance, not lack. Generous people live to bless others through liberal giving.

A person with a generous spirit is gracious, magnanimous, and looks at life through the eyes of abundance, not lack. Generous people live to bless others.

The Word of God encourages and rewards generosity.

*He who is generous will be blessed, for he gives some of his food to the poor.*
— Proverbs 22:9

*He who is gracious (generous) to a poor man lends to the Lord, and He will repay Him for his good deed.*
— Proverbs 19:17

*He has given freely (generously) to the poor; His righteousness endures forever, His horn will be exalted in honor.*
— Psalm 112: 9

*Blessed is he that considers the poor, the Lord will deliver him in time of trouble.*
— Psalm 41:1

*Now this I say, he who sows sparingly shall also reap sparingly; and he who sows bountifully (generously) shall also reap bountifully.*
— 2 Corinthians 9:6

*There is one who scatters, yet increases all the more, and there is one who withholds what is justly due, but it results only in want. The generous man will be prosperous, and he who waters will himself be watered.*
— Proverbs 11:24-25

According to the above Scriptures, the generous man is the blessed man. The one who looks out for others and gives generously to those in need is the person who will be blessed with prosperity.

Generosity is a choice. You choose to scatter or to withhold God's gifts. I decide to have a closed or open hand. Stingy and cursed, or generous and blessed, it's up to you.

> Generosity is a choice. You choose to scatter or to withhold God's gifts.

Good servants and stewards of Christ are generous with God's gifts. Why? Because God has been generous with them. To be Christ-like is to be gracious and generous in giving.

## Generous or Stingy?

1. When it comes to giving, are you a generous person? If so, cite some recent evidence that supports your liberality with God's gifts.

   _____

   _____

   _____

   _____

   _____

2. Would those who know you describe you as a generous person?

_____

_____

_____

_____

_____

3. Who do you know currently that could be blessed by a generous act on your part towards them? What is their situation? What do they need?

_____

_____

_____

_____

_____

_____

4. How do you plan to show them God's goodness through you?

_____

_____

_____

_____

_____

_____

## THINK IT OVER

God made the sun — it gives.

God made the moon — it gives.

God made the stars — they give.

God made the air — it gives.

God made the clouds — they give.

God made the earth — it gives.

God made the sea — it gives.

God made the trees — they give.

God made the flowers — they give.

God made the birds — they give.

God made the animals — they give.

God made the plan — He gives.

God made man — He ...........?

*Author unknown*

# Lesson 9

## Managing Your Time

*Be careful how you walk, not as unwise men, but as wise, making the most of your time, because the days are evil. So then do not be foolish, but understand what the will of the Lord is.*
— Ephesians 5:15-17

*Teach us to number our days, that we may present to Thee a heart of wisdom.*
— Psalm 90:12

### PRINCIPLES
- Count each day because each day counts.
- Successful people are in control of their time.
- God doesn't ask us to do more than He gives us the time to do.

### PURPOSE
Our goal is to understand how valuable time is. You will discover that your time is, in actuality, God's time. Because time is so important, it must be redeemed. Redeeming time requires skillful management of the limited, fleeting moments entrusted to you. The proper, productive management of time underlies all other stewardship strategies for successful living. If you don't manage time well, you won't manage anything else well either. You will also identify common time stealers and counter them with common sense time stretchers.

Wise use of time will be of great benefit to you and your fellow man. Successful stewardship of time will also bring glory to God.

### DISCUSSION
Time. What does time mean to you? Many years ago, Sir Walter Raleigh made this remark about time: "Dost thou love life? Then do not squander time. For that's the stuff life is made of."

Life is made up of time. Every event under the sun as well as everything we experience is measured in some way or other by time. In Ecclesiastes 3:1, Solomon gives us God's take on time: There is an appointed time for everything. And there is a time for everything under heaven.

*Because time is so important, it must be redeemed. Redeeming time requires skillful management of the limited, fleeting moments entrusted to you.*

God has appointed a time for everything in life. A detailed look at Ecclesiastes 3:2-8 will reveal that there is "a time to live, and a time to die. A time to laugh, and a time to cry. A time to be silent, and a time to speak up. A time to love, a time to hate. A time to tear down, and a time to build up" and so on. There is a season or time for everything.

Not only is there an appointed time for everything, there is also an appropriate time for everything. Verse 11 says: He (God) has made everything appropriate in its time. He has also set eternity in their hearts.

Everything has its moment in time and every moment is important. Our Creator ties time and eternity together. Though eternity is timeless, the way we use time here on earth affects how we will spend eternity. If we waste our time on trivial pursuits and miss the mark by not coming to know God, eternity with Him in heaven will not be our reward. On the other hand, if we value time, use it wisely, and pursue God until we find, embrace, and live for Him, we will spend eternity in heaven with our Maker and Redeemer. That's a wise use of our time here on earth.

Wise King Solomon knew time is invaluable and indispensable. Because this is scripturally true, it is extremely important that we value time. Too many people take time for granted. Time is the stuff of life. We must recognize the supreme importance of time. We must also realize that managing time well is critical to loving and enjoying life. If we squander or waste time, we waste our lives and miss the enjoyment that life can offer.

> Wasting time is wasting life. Once time passes, it's history. It can never be retrieved.

Wasting time is wasting life. Once time passes it's history. It can never be retrieved.

When I was young, I thought that I had all the time in the world. Time, in my youth, seemed to pass so slowly. The hands on the clock couldn't move fast enough, especially when I was sitting in a stuffy classroom listening to a boring teacher. I was always in a hurry for time to hurry up so I would be grown up and could live my life the way I wanted to.

Now that I am grown and living life the way I choose, time is moving much too quickly! I catch myself wishing that time would slow down. Isn't that ironic?

Scripture puts the swift passage of time in perspective for us. Ecclesiastes 12:1 exhorts us to "remember also your Creator in the days of your youth, before the evil days come and the years draw near when you will say, 'I have no delight in them.'" Though this verse seems to be a bit on the depressive side, it really isn't.

The writer is simply saying that when you are young in years, learn to recognize and honor your Creator. Life has a way of sneaking up on you. Days rapidly turn into years and years into a lifetime. With each passing day you will be glad that you learned to walk with God when you were young.

St. Augustine of Hippo said "time never takes time off." Time really does fly when you're having fun — and growing older! According to 1 Chronicles 29:15, Job 7:6, 8:9, 9:25, 14:2, Psalm 39:5, Isaiah 38:12, and James 4:14 time is short. Life, at best, is brief in duration.

Time is valuable as well as short. The following verses tell us that we should never fall into the subtle trap of presumption regarding time and opportunity. We should guard against thinking that time will last forever and opportunity will always knock.

> *Do not boast about tomorrow, for you do not know what a day may bring forth.*
> — Proverbs 27:1

> *"Come," they say, "let us get wine, and let us drink heavily of strong drink; and tomorrow will be like today, only more so."*
> — Isaiah 56:12

> *Do not put off the day of calamity, and would you bring near the seat of violence?*
> — Amos 6:3

> *I will say to my soul, "Soul, you have many goods laid up for many years to come; take your ease, eat, drink, and be merry."*
> — Luke 12:19

> *As he was discussing righteousness, self-control and the judgment to come, Felix became frightened and said, "Go away for the present, and when I find time, I will summon you."*
> — Acts 24:25

> *Come now, you who say, "Today or tomorrow, we shall go to such and such a city, and spend a year there and engage in business and make a profit." Yet you do not know what your life will be like tomorrow. You are just a vapor that appears for a little while and them vanishes away.*
> — James 4:13-14

We should guard against thinking that time will last forever and opportunity will always knock.

Summarize the main thoughts from those verses:

_____

_____

The Bible makes it clear that we have no guarantee of living another day. Tomorrow may never come. We hope it will, but we have no certainty. The time frame we have to deal with is today. Now is what matters. That is why it is imperative that we be serious minded about making today count.

> To succeed in life we must make wise use of our time. Wise use of time means that we understand the value of a day.

To succeed in life we must make wise use of our time. Wise use of time means that we understand the value of a day.

David tells us in Psalm 90:12 to do what concerning our days (time)?

_____

_____

What kind of heart are we to present to God?

_____

_____

What does a day mean to you? How important is today to God? How important is today to you?

_____

_____

The Psalmist exhorts us to "number our days." That means to count our time. Notice that we learn from God ("So teach us") how to accomplish this. The Lord Himself instructs His students regarding counting their days and making their days count. Without His able assistance, we would miss the importance of every day.

A heart of wisdom from God views life this way: Don't let days slip by without noticing how valuable they are. Carefully number every single day. Each tick of the clock (86,000 seconds every twenty-four hours) is a God-given opportunity to gain wisdom. Don't waste one second. Respect time. Make it work for you. Live each day fully aware that time is more valuable than any other thing you possess. Then you will prove yourself wise before God.

While time marches relentlessly on, some people foolishly choose to waste it while others wisely choose to manage it. Wise hearts don't waste time. Using time wisely is a sign of wisdom.

# Our Time Is His Time

Who does your time belong to, anyway? We talk and act as if time belongs to us. We don't want people "wasting our time," "encroaching upon our time," "controlling our time," or "stealing our time," but a careful reading of Psalm 31:14-15 reveals that our time is not really our time:

> As for me, I trust in Thee, O Lord, I say, "Thou art my God." My times are in Thy hands.

David openly acknowledged His personal faith in God. He trusted that his times (meaning seasons, events, and experiences of life) were in someone else's hands. Seasons in life are measured and bound by time. In other words, times are made up of time. It stands to reason that if our times are in God's hands, so is our time. Both come from His gracious, holy hand.

Time is a precious gift from our heavenly Father. Like everything in His created universe, time belongs to Him. He is the originator and owner of time. Our time and times, are not ours, but His.

The time that we have to use is a trust from God. God entrusts this time to our care. It is His. We are stewards and managers of that time. Remember, stewards are required to be found faithful in the management of God's resources. That includes time.

What are you doing with God's time?

*Time is a precious gift from our Heavenly Father. Like everything in His created universe, time belongs to Him. He is the originator and owner of time. Our time and times, are not ours, but His.*

# Time Is to Be Redeemed

Wise men make the most of their God-given time. Addressing the vital importance of walking in wisdom in this evil world, Paul instructed the Ephesian believers to make the most of their time.

> Be careful how you walk, not as unwise men, but as wise, making the most of your time, because the days are evil. So then do not be foolish, but understand what the will of the Lord is.
> — Ephesians 5:15-17

As their father in the faith, Paul was properly concerned about how his spiritual children were living their lives. Christians are to be wise. They are to walk, or conduct themselves, carefully in this world. A careful walk (the word *circumspect* is used in the KING JAMES VERSION) means to look around, walk strictly, straightly, and without stumbling. The Greek word for circumspect carries the idea of precision and accuracy. Christians must see to it that they walk carefully, with exactness.

In THE TWENTIETH CENTURY NEW TESTAMENT, verse 15 says, "Take great care, then, how you live." The PHILLIPS translation reads "Live life, then, with a due sense of responsibility." GOODSPEED says, "Do not act thoughtlessly, but like sensible men." The opposite would be to walk carelessly and without proper guidance, with no forethought. The Christian walk cannot and must not be left to chance or guesswork. Believers must make wise decisions and at all times seek to do God's will.

In verse 14, Paul is telling his fellow believers, "Wake up. Do not sleepwalk. Open your eyes wide. Make it your aim to make the most of your day. Don't be foolish. Walk in wisdom." It's too bad that in Paul's day and in ours we find that many professing Christians just drift through life, like they are sleepwalking. Asleep on their spiritual feet, they don't make the most of the opportunities before them to live for the Lord and serve Him. They show themselves unwise. How does this happen? They don't realize the importance of the times they live in and of the time God has given them. Unwise men don't make the most of their time. They fail to understand the Will of the Lord for their lives.

In the KING JAMES VERSION, verse 16 includes the words "redeeming the time, for the days are evil." The same basic thought is found in Colossians 4:5, which reads "walk in wisdom towards them that are without, redeeming the time." In biblical terms, "redeem" means "to buy back" or "buy up." Jesus redeemed us, or bought us back from sin and death. "Buying back" connotates the idea of making the most of an opportunity, especially for good. That's what Jesus did for us. His sacrificial death on the Cross paid the price to buy us back from the devil, and provided the opportunity for us to be saved and go to heaven.

Read the following translations of verse 16 from various biblical commentators. Let the thought of making the most of your time and opportunity sink into your spirit.

BARCLAY: Use your time with all economy.

ALFORD: Buying up opportunities.

PHILLIPS: Make the best use of your time, despite all the difficulties of these days.

NEW ENGLISH BIBLE: Use the present opportunity to the full.

JERUSALEM BIBLE: This may be a wicked age, but your lives should redeem it.

LIVING BIBLE: Make the most of every opportunity for doing good.

> The Christian walk cannot and must not be left to chance or guesswork. Believers must make wise decisions and at all times seek to do God's will.

I once heard a preacher say that this verse means "to rescue or recover our time from waste, to improve it for great and important purposes." That's hitting the nail on the head!

Christians need to recover their time from being wasted. Because time is short, the days we live in are difficult. Opportunities to do good pass quickly if we are not careful. We must use time for great purposes. Our English word "opportunity" comes from the Latin and means "toward the port." It suggests a ship taking advantage of the wind and tide to arrive safely in the harbor. The ship sails while it has opportunity — favorable wind and tide. The briefness of life and the limited time we have provides a strong argument for making the best use of the opportunities God gives us. In other words, we need to set our sails when the tide is up and the wind is blowing favorably.

Christians are to redeem time and make the most of it.

Wise or unwise? Foolish or understanding concerning God's will? Which you are is dictated by how you use your time. Unwise, foolish people mismanage their time. They don't realize how vital it is to buy back time and every opportunity for good that God has given them.

The wise person Paul refers to here is the person who comes to understand God's will in these last days. This person knows the days are evil, and makes the most of their time and opportunities. A wise walk as a Christian is measured in a large part by his/her use of time. Believers who know that their time is actually His time will be careful in accounting for their stewardship of time.

> Christians need to recover their time from being wasted. Because time is short, the days we live in are difficult. Opportunities to do good pass quickly if we are not careful. We must use time for great purposes.

## Time Stealers

Time is packed with potential for immense good. Our archenemy, the devil, knows that time is opportunity. His objective and ultimate goal is to prevent God's people from doing good and walking in wisdom these last days. Satan spares no effort in trying to steal our time.

Other "thieves" will rob us of opportunity for doing good, if given the chance. Walking in wisdom means clearly and confidently recognizing who these thieves are, realizing what they are up to, and with Christ's help, consistently resisting their relentless assault on our time.

## Laziness Steals Time

We are as lazy as our circumstances allow us to be. Admittedly we live in an age obsessed with leisure and comfort. Increasingly America is evolving into a very laid back, sedentary society. If we would be honest with ourselves, sometimes leisure is just a new-fangled word for plain old laziness. How much time is wasted because people choose to be lazy? Laziness steals time and opportunity in a flash.

Proverbs 18:9, 19:5, 22:13, 24:30-31, Ecclesiastes 10:18, 2 Thessalonians 3:11, and Hebrews 6:12 describe the plight of the slothful (lazy) in life.

_____

_____

_____

What is God telling us in these verses?

_____

_____

_____

If heaven is a place of rest, many people should be all practiced up for it!

Lazy people fail in life because they lose time instead of using time. They rarely, if ever, enter through the door marked opportunity!

Think about it! The last time you had a lazy spell, what happened to the possibilities within the time you lost? What opportunity for accomplishing something worthwhile was lost forever because you succumbed to a spirit of laziness?

## Overcoming Laziness

When you are tempted to be lazy, make a conscious effort to resist the impulse immediately. Expend the necessary energy to repulse laziness. Remind yourself that incredible opportunities are lost forever when you curl up on the couch and choose to do nothing with the precious time you have. There is nothing wrong with a restful nap once in a while. Naps are necessary for refreshment and renewal. But when short naps turn into long spells of laziness, we invite a thief into our life.

Get off the sofa. Fight slothfulness in Jesus' name. Kick the spirit of laziness and his slothful siblings out the front door. Lock the entrance to your mind and heart against the spirit of laziness.

We are as lazy as our circumstances allow us to be. Admittedly we live in an age obsessed with leisure and comfort.

## Idleness Steals Time

Few things are more dangerous to a person's character than having nothing to do and plenty of time in which to do it. People with nothing but time on their hands get into trouble. Idleness is, indeed, the devil's playground. Satan's strategy is to isolate the idle person and keep him out of the flow of life-generating activity. The devil searches for idle hands that he can bind up with a spirit of inactivity. Inactivity is a mortal enemy of time.

> *By much slothfulness the building decayeth; and through idleness of the hands the house droppeth through.*
> — Ecclesiastes 10:18 KJV

According to the above verse, what happens to the house when the owner's hands are idle?

_____

_____

_____

What do you think idle hands are?

_____

_____

_____

Describe a time when you were in an idle mode.

_____

_____

_____

How did you feel about being idle? What did you accomplish while you were idle?

_____

_____

_____

_____

Idleness is, indeed, the devil's playground. Satan's strategy is to isolate the idle person and keep him out of the flow of life-generating activity.

The word *idle* means "lacking worth or basis; useless, not occupied or employed; not turned to appropriate use; inactive." Thus, when we are idle, we are inactive, worthless, useless, and are not doing what we were created to do. Ouch! According to the Bible, we are wired by God to be active, useful, and to accomplish something worthwhile.

Because we are Christians, something in us should detest idleness. Every fiber of our redeemed beings should scream out against being useless and worthless. Jesus saved us to serve and do good works! Ephesians 2:10 says we are His workmanship, created in Christ Jesus for good works, which God prepared beforehand, that we should walk in them.

We are to walk in good works. Walking denotes activity, not idleness or inactivity. We are His workmanship, created by Him to be busy doing good works for the Kingdom. To sit idly by, accomplishing nothing worthwhile is definitely not God's will for a believer. He did not do a work in us for us not to work!

Idleness robs us of God's high and holy purpose for our lives. It is also a serious waste of precious time. When our hands are idle, Satan's aren't. He picks time from our pockets.

## Overcoming Idleness

Determine to be an active Christian. Discipline yourself to keep busy with the good works God has prepared for you. Dedicate your life to accomplishing worthwhile endeavors. Direct your energy to assisting others escaping the snare of idleness and inactivity. Be pro-active and assertive in your battle against idleness.

When the spirit of idleness knocks on your door, make sure nobody is home. Get out and experience life. Use your hands to help someone else improve their situation.

## Procrastination Steals Time

To procrastinate means to put off until tomorrow what we should do today. How easy it is for our fickle flesh to fall into this trap. The devil is thrilled when we postpone what God wants us to do. He knows if we don't obey God today, there is a high probability we won't obey Him tomorrow either.

Most people have plenty of experience when it comes to procrastination. We say we want to get in better physical shape, but we'll exercise later. We say we want to lose weight so we decide to diet. But then we tell ourselves there is no harm in a few extra calories today. We can always diet tomorrow. We have all been there and done that.

Procrastination is that intrusive, nagging urge that prompts and pushes us to excuse ourselves from present responsibilities. Look up the following

Idleness robs us of God's high and holy purpose for our lives. It is also a serious waste of precious time. When our hands are idle, Satan's aren't. He picks time from our pockets.

examples of procrastination in the Bible. Take careful note of the consequences experienced by people when they put off what they should have done.

| | |
|---|---|
| Israel seeking to enter the Promised Land. | Numbers 11:40-45 |
| Saul repenting of his disobedience | 1 Samuel 15: 24-26 |
| Israel repenting of sin. | Jeremiah 8:20 |
| The virgins preparing for the coming of the Bridegroom | Matthew 25:11-12 |

According to God's Word, some of the causes of procrastination are worldly entanglements (Genesis 19:16), family cares (Matthew 8:21 and Luke 9:61), unbelief (Acts 17:32), and personal convenience (Acts 24:25).

Dennis Waitley, in his book *Being The Best* says this about procrastination.

> When I am caught up in opportunity-stifling behavior, such as scapegoating or trying to love risk-free, one of my favorite 'hiding places' is procrastination. When I procrastinate, I never do today what I can put off until tomorrow — or maybe next week. Of course, I pay a heavy price. When I procrastinate, I have this gnawing feeling of being fatigued, always behind. I try to tell myself that I am actually taking it easy and gathering my energies for a new big push, but procrastination is another weaver of myths and lies. The truth is, procrastination doesn't save me time or energy; it drains away both and leaves me with self-doubt and self delusion.

Fear is at the root of procrastination. It may be fear of failure, or fear of success. Who doesn't want to put off failure until tomorrow? Besides, by tomorrow or next week or next month maybe something will change. And success could mean more responsibilities.

Procrastination hurts us in two ways. First, we waste valuable time and energy putting off what we should be doing. Second, we then have to use more time and energy making up for what we could have already done! Procrastination is a no win situation. Satan knows it!

Benjamin Franklin showed great insight when he said, "You may delay, but time will not."

Jeremiah 8:20 is a haunting reminder of the opportunity that procrastination steals from us: Harvest is past, summer is ended, and we are not saved.

Have you ever missed something important because you procrastinated? Procrastination is the grave in which opportunity is buried.

Fear is at the root of procrastination. It may be fear of failure, or fear of success.

## Overcoming Procrastination

Alexander the Great, on being asked how he had conquered the world, replied, "By not delaying."

In 2 Corinthians 6:1-2 Paul had a few words to say about conquering procrastination.

> *Working together with Him, we also urge you not to receive the grace of God in vain — for He says, "at the acceptable time I listened to you, and on the day of salvation I helped you. behold, now is the acceptable time, behold, now is the day of salvation."*

Now is always God's time. Because time is His, we should view time the same way He does, and not postpone until tomorrow what we can do today!

Doing it now will defeat procrastination every time. Where would you be today if Jesus had procrastinated and put off dying on the Cross for your sins?

## Distraction Steals Time

The Christian life is one of focus. In Philippians 3:7-17, Paul makes clear what believers in Christ are to pursue. In verse 13, he literally reduced his life to "this one thing I do." Paul used time well because he was focused. Because he knew what he was supposed to do, he spent his time doing it.

Throughout its sacred pages, Scripture directs God's people to be focused. We are to look directly ahead; be single-minded; never turn to the right or left. We are to keep our eyes "fixed on Jesus" (Hebrews 12:1-3). The Lord is our focal point. He is our example for keeping straight and true to God's will. He accomplished His earthly mission because He resisted the powers of distraction around Him. The devil, religious hypocrites, traditions of men, societal and cultural expectations, the Roman empire, and the temptations of His own flesh tried to steer the Lord off course, to distract Him from His holy calling. But His goal was Calvary. Nothing deterred Him from the Cross.

Use time for things that outlast time.

If ever people at any time in history were tempted to distraction, it's today. Everywhere we turn, something or someone vies for our attention, time, energy, and resources. The spirit of distraction abounds. Its goal is to confuse us, to keep us running in endless circles, never to stay our course and accomplish God's will. Distraction, by its very nature, eats up valuable time.

Now is always God's time. Because time is His, we should view time the same way He does, and not postpone until tomorrow what we can do today!

Focus makes the most of time. Distraction destroys time and the precious opportunities time provides.

## PERSONAL EVALUATION

1. Are you easily distracted? If so, why?

   _____

   _____

   _____

2. What kinds of things distract you the most?

   _____

   _____

   _____

3. Name a time when distraction got you off course. What did you lose because you were distracted? How much time did you have to make up to overcome your loss?

   _____

   _____

### Overcoming Distraction

Make a decision to stay focused. Decide what your "one thing" is and do it. Look straight ahead every day. Say "no" to everything that attempts to distract you and derail you from your goals. Remove anything from your life that is a distraction.

Make a decision to stay focused. Decide what your "one thing" is and do it. Look straight ahead every day.

# Time Stretchers

Someone once said that the most effective time in many people's lives is the week before vacation! There is a ring of truth in that statement, isn't there?

Two truths concerning time are very apparent in life: The man who makes the best use of his time has the most to spare. Those who make the worst use of their time are usually the ones who complain of never having enough time.

Everyone receives the same twenty-four hours each day. No one receives more; no one receives less. Keeping that unchangeable, inescapable fact in mind, what is it that separates those who don't have enough time and those who have time to spare?

Successful time management is the dividing line. How we choose to use our time makes all the difference in the world. It is the difference between winning and losing, being usable or unusable, being fruitful or unfruitful.

Faithful management stretches time. We find we have more than enough time to do what God has called us to do when we are diligent to manage time well. The following practical suggestions will help you learn to manage your time better if you will apply them to your daily life.

1. Pray and Plan. Many Christians simply do not plan their day before God.
2. Prioritize your day. Put things in order of importance.
3. First things first. Tackle urgent issues right away.
4. Difficult things first. Resist the urge to avoid unpleasant tasks.
5. Complete things first. Finish unfinished projects.
6. To-do list. Work from a "to do" list with deadlines. Keep your deadlines.
7. Select and reject. Be courageous enough to say "yes" or "no" to demands on your time.
8. Do your homework. Find out what you need to know to succeed.
9. Delegate. Have others help you accomplish your mission.
10. Evaluate your day. At the end of each day, note how you did. Resolve to improve tomorrow.

What would happen if we applied the above ten time management principles to every week of our lives? Increased productivity for certain, and you would probably sleep better at night too!

In John 9:4 Jesus said, "We must work the works of Him who sent me, as long as it is day; night is coming when no man can work." What did He mean? Jesus meant God's work is very important. Opportunities to work for Him are limited, so we need to do His work while we have time. Reflecting upon His short three-year ministry on earth and what was accomplished, Jesus was a master of time management.

> Opportunities to work for Him are limited, so we need to do His work while we have time.... Jesus was a master of time management.

## APPLICATION

1. Are you a good manager or a poor manager of God's time? Qualify your answer.

   _____

   _____


2. Which time stealers have picked your pocket? What can you do to close the door on these thieves?

   _____

   _____

3. Evaluate a typical week in your life. How much of your time is devoted to yourself? To God and His work? In service and ministry to others? What do you do with leisure time?

_____

_____

4. Do you think you have spare time, or not enough time?

_____

_____

5. Make a list of the ten ways you can stretch your time. Honestly evaluate yourself in each area. Write out a personalized plan for improving your time management.

_____

_____

# A Word on Time and God's Timing

In 1 Thessalonians 5:24 we find these encouraging words from Paul, "Faithful is He who calls you, and He will bring it to pass."

It is wonderfully reassuring to know that when God calls us to do His will, He is faithful to bring His will to pass! We can count on Him to provide all that we need to succeed. The pressure is on God, not us. We don't bring our calling to pass, He does. Where God guides He provides. God's will allows time for completion. The Lord is faithful to provide the time we need to accomplish His plan for our lives. There is always enough time to do God's will.

The devil pressures us with time. He tries to convince us that there isn't enough time to see our dreams come true, our plans completed, or our hopes and desires come to pass. This is one of his best tricks. But ask yourself this question. What kind of a heavenly Father would God be if He called His children to do things and knew there wasn't enough time to do them?

That's not the God of the Bible. God loves us and provides enough time for us to carry out His will. Every time.

God also understands the power of timing. "Timing is everything" is a well-known success principle. God does not separate time and timing. They work together for our good.

*The pressure is on God, not us. We don't bring our calling to pass, He does. Where God guides He provides.*

Study 1 Samuel 1:20; Psalm 1:3, 105:19; Ecclesiastes 3:1 and 11; Daniel 9:24; Mark 11:15; Galatians 4:4, 6:9; Ephesians 1:10; 1 Timothy 6:14-15, 2:6; Titus 1:3; Hebrews 9:26; and 1 Peter 5:6. In these verses you will find phrases such as "in the fullness of time," "appointed time," "appropriate time," "due season," "right time," "due time," and "proper time." As you study what transpired in these passages, one thing is clear: God is always on time. He is never in a hurry. He is never late. Perfect timing fits the nature and character of God. The proper time is His time. He knows at what point in time everything He has designed for us is to take place. Timing is everything in God's Kingdom.

Years ago during a trying transition, I found myself becoming increasingly frustrated with the issue of timing. It seemed to me that important things I was trusting God for should have been manifesting themselves sooner then they were. I was fast becoming impatient with the process. Has this ever happened to you? One day, as I prayed to the Lord, the Spirit of God spoke to me: "Steve, be at peace with My pace."

What a timely word to my impatience! That revelation revolutionized my thinking and transformed my attitude about trusting God's processes. God taught me that His pace might vary. Sometimes slow, sometimes fast. Sometimes time seems to stand still. No matter. I can trust Him. His timing is perfect for me. By accepting this fact of Kingdom life, I have learned to run my race at His pace.

When we decide to be at peace with God's pace, we are making a powerful statement of faith: God, I trust You with Your time and timing in my life.

He provides adequate time for accomplishing His will. Our primary responsibility is to manage the time He gives us wisely. Faithful stewards understand that success in life results from a lifestyle of managing time in a trustworthy manner.

> Perfect timing fits the nature and character of God. The proper time is His time. He knows at what point in time everything He has designed for us is to take place. Timing is everything in God's Kingdom.

VALUING TIME
I have just a little minute,
Only sixty seconds in it,
Forced upon me, cannot refuse it.
Did not seek it, did not choose it,
But it is up to me to use it.
I must suffer if I abuse it;
Just a tiny, little minute,
But eternity is in it.
— *Anonymous*

# Lesson 10

## Managing Your Talent

*As each one has received a special gift, employ it in serving one another, as good stewards of the manifold grace of God.*
— 1 Peter 4:10

*Whether then you eat or drink, or whatever you do, do all to the glory of God.*
— 1 Corinthians 10:31

### PRINCIPLES
- Every person has received unique abilities and talents as gifts from God.
- Gifts are to be used for the glory of God and the good of men.
- Excel at what you do well.

### PURPOSE
God is gracious and good when it comes to giving us gifts. In the natural and spiritual realm, we have been blessed with talent. We are responsible for managing the intelligence, aptitudes, disposition, abilities, and gifts that God has given us. A lifestyle that manages our various talents contributes greatly to our personal success.

In this lesson we will discuss how God has gifted us, what we are to do with our gifts, and how the proper stewardship of God-given gifts glorifies God and benefits others.

### DISCUSSION
Have you ever given serious thought as to how God gets things done? Especially on earth? Does He just snap His fingers and presto, it's done? Does He speak a word, dispatch a squadron of angels, send email, or what? We have a pretty good grasp of how humans do things. But how does the Creator of the universe accomplish his will and plan? In what manner is the Lord's redemptive agenda carried out in the human arena?

Through people. God uses people to perform and complete His purposes.

A careful reading of Psalm 139 reveals how special and unique every human being is. In verse 3 David wrote that God "is intimately acquainted with all my ways." The Creator knows every minute, intimate detail about everyone.

> We are responsible for managing the intelligence, aptitudes, disposition, abilities, and gifts that God has given us. A lifestyle that manages our various talents contributes greatly to our personal success.

That means the Creator is vitally interested and involved in the lives of His creatures whom He lovingly and purposefully created in His own image.

David's inspired words flow on as he writes in verses 13-18 about how wonderfully unique we are.

> *Thou didst form my inward parts; Thou didst weave me in my mother's womb. I will give thanks to Thee, for I am fearfully and wonderfully made; Wonderful are Thy works, and my soul knows it very well. My frame was not hidden from Thee, when I was made in secret, and skillfully wrought in the depths of the earth. Thine eyes have seen my unformed substance; and in Thy book they were all written, the days that were ordained for me, when as yet there was not one of them. How precious also are Thy thoughts to me, O God! How vast is the sum of them! If I should count them, they would outnumber the sand. When I awake, I am still with Thee.*

As my pastor often says, it's time to put your shouting clothes on! Talk about uplifting, spirit-inspiring words! By affirming how special we are, this psalm builds and reinforces self-esteem and self-worth. Think for a moment about what David really said.

Almighty God thinks about us all the time. He is thinking about you this very moment! He wrote down every day of your life — before they even existed. He was present in the secret places and actively involved when you were "fearfully and wonderfully made." His eyes saw your unformed substance, then, His creative hands gave you substance in the form of a uniquely, individualistic person. Of the multiple billions of people who have populated planet earth thus far, no two share the same fingerprint!

There is nobody like you, and there never will be. The mold is broken after each person is created and blessed with their uniqueness. I'm special. You're special. We're all special! Now that's something worth shouting about!

We come from the same Creator, but each human being is different. What sets people apart from one another? What defines their differences? Their gifts. The individual abilities and talents they possess distinguish them from other people. Solomon tells us that a person's gifts and the skillful use of those gifts sets them apart from others.

> *A man's gift makes room for him and takes him before great men.*
> — Proverbs 18:16

*Do you see a man skilled in his work? He will stand before kings; he will not stand before obscure men.*
— Proverbs 22:29

Our place in life, where each of us fits in the human drama, is determined by our unique, God-given gifts. Our talents (gifts and abilities) take us to the places and positions God has ordained for us. Gifts make room for us so we can fulfill his will and make the most of the opportunities He gives us for doing good. You are special and specially gifted. That means God has something very special for you to do!

## Biblical Truth About Talent: 1 Peter 4:10-11

Peter believed the end of all things was near. (See 2 Peter 3:1-3.) His two books were written to help Christians successfully witness for Christ as time, as he knew it, was winding down. The temptation for some believers was to view the end times as the opportunity to behave like a hermit and pull back from life as they awaited the Lord's much-anticipated, triumphant return. Their attitude was "sit back, relax, and wait for Jesus."

No rocking chair for this apostle. Peter's brand of Christianity was active. His epistles constitute a rallying cry to God's soldiers. A faith-stirring message that could be entitled "Be a Helper, Not a Hermit." His passionate exhortation to his fellow Christians was for them to serve people with the gifts God had given them. Peter urged his brethren to be faithful to minister to men in such a way that they would be benefited and God would be glorified.

The following translations of 1 Peter 4:10 clarify and amplify these thoughts.

*Each one, as good managers of God's different gifts, must use it for the good of others; the special gift he has received from God.*
— TEV

*Whatever gift each of you may have received, use it to serve one another, like good stewards, dispensing the grace of God in its varied form.*
— NEB

We can see four very important truths in this verse concerning the management of our talents.

## 1. Everyone in the Body of Christ Is Talented or Gifted

Note that Peter specifically says "each one has received." Every member of the body of Christ has been gifted for service. According to 1 Corinthians 12, the church is one body with multiple members (See verse 20.). Each member is vital, critical to the proper functioning of the body. Each member with their gifts is indispensable to the success of the body of Christ's ministry to a lost world.

Tyndale remarks in his commentary: "Peter implies that every Christian has received some gift from God, a gift which is to be held in trust for the benefit of the whole church and is to be exercised for the ministry, for the good of others."

Commenting on this passage, William Barclay says: "The Church needs every gift that a man has. It may be the gift of speaking, of music, of the ability to visit people. It may be a craft or skill, which can be used, in the practical service of the Church. It may be a house, which a man possesses, or money, which he has inherited. There is no gift that cannot be placed at the service of Christ."

God equips each member of His household for service.

Natural and spiritual gifts are for all, not just a few. Many erroneously think that gifts and talents in the body of Christ are for the professional ministers only. Nothing could be further from the truth. The church does not have gifted and ungifted people. "Each one" of us has received a special gift from God.

"Each one" includes you. Don't ever let anyone tell you you don't have talent!

Think about it. You are so special to God that He has chosen to give you gifts for successful living and ministry.

## 2. Talents Are Special Gifts from God

Man does not gift himself. The source of gifts is God. He is the giver, and we are the receiver! First Corinthians 12:11 and 18 read: "But one and the same Spirit works all these things, distributing to each one individually, just as He wills...." But now God has placed the members (with their gifts), each one of them, in the body, just as he desired. God, not men, determines talents, or gifts. They are distributed individually, not assembly line style. You are gifted, not according to your will or desires, but according to God's will and desire for you.

God gives gifts; we receive them. Adam Clarke said, "Whatever gifts or endowments any man may possess, they are, properly speaking, not his own. They are the Lord's property and to be employed in His work, and to promote His glory!"

*Natural and spiritual gifts are for all, not just a few. Many erroneously think that gifts and talents in the body of Christ are for the professional ministers only. Nothing could be further from the truth. The church does not have gifted and ungifted people. "Each one" of us has received a special gift from God.*

Your gifts are God's gift to you. They belong to Him even though He has graciously entrusted them to you.

The NASV says "as each one has received a special gift…." God in His grace has provided special gifts for special people. The gifts we possess are tailor made for us, unique and individual. Because they are specially designed to fit each individual, no gift is greater than another. All gifts are valuable and necessary.

Study 1 Corinthians 12:12-24. Read it in various translations if you have them available.

How important are all the various members of the body of Christ?

_____
_____
_____

According to Paul, why can't a person say a particular gift is unimportant?

_____
_____
_____
_____

What does the apostle Paul say about the "less honorable" members in the body of Christ? (vv. 20-24)

_____
_____
_____

If the "less honorable" members are given "abundant honor," it seems to reason that every member with their differing gifts is special and important.

_____
_____
_____

God's gifts are special!

Your gifts are God's gift to you. They belong to Him even though He has graciously entrusted them to you.

What do you think God thinks when we whine or gripe about our gifts? How does He feel when we compare our gifts to others' and then complain that we wish we had what they have? Do you think it might break God's heart when His children are ungrateful for the special gifts He has given them? What does God want us to think and feel about His gifts to us?

_____

_____

_____

_____

Write a paragraph thanking God for your gifts.

_____

_____

_____

_____

### 3. Gifts (Talents and Abilities) Are Given for Serving Others

Why are gifts given, anyway? Peter says gifts are given for service. The Christian life is, above all else, a life of service. Our God-given gifts are to be employed, put to work, in serving other people. Christianity is a full-service religion. There should be no unemployed servant in the body of Christ. Unused gifts are wasted opportunities to do good to others and make a lasting impact for the Kingdom of God.

Jesus set the standard for serving and giving. See Matthew 20:20-26. As the Servant of servants, He was the most gifted and talented person Who ever lived. Neither His faith nor His gifts were limited in anyway. He fulfilled the Father's will because He employed His gifts and talents in serving others.

*The word serving used in 1 Peter 4:10 is a general word used throughout the New Testament. It includes all kinds of service to people.*

The word *serving* used in 1 Peter 4:10 is a general word used throughout the New Testament. It includes all kinds of service to people. For instance, in Acts 6:1-4 this word is used in reference to both serving others through ministry of the Word (preaching and teaching) and ministry of food (waiting tables and serving widows) — sharing Scripture with a congregation and scooping potatoes on the plates of hungry people are equal ministries in the sight of God.

# Gifts Are Tools

Gifts, like tools, are necessary in order to do a job. Imagine a contractor who agrees to build his friend a house and then shows up at the work site with an empty toolbox! How can a carpenter construct a house without tools? Seems ridiculous, doesn't it? The same can be said of believers who are called and equipped to serve but don't bring their equipment to the ministry site. They have neglected to use the natural and spiritual gifts (tools) in their "toolbox" in order to get the ministry job done.

Gifts are to use and share. Talent from God is not something to be hoarded. God's gifts are to be used to help people. They are not for bragging, but are for bringing the Good News to people. Though gifts bless us, talent is not just for our own benefit. Gifts, when viewed Biblically, are to benefit others.

> *Do nothing from selfishness or empty conceit, but with humility of mind let each of you regard one another as more important than himself; do not merely look out for your own personal interests, but also for the interests of others.*
> — Philippians 2:3-4

When was the last time you used your gifts to serve someone else?

## 4. Good Stewards Use Their Gifts for God's Glory

Gifts, like every other God-given resource in life, are to be managed faithfully. Note that Peter says we are to serve as "good stewards." We saw earlier that the Today's English Version calls those who serve with their gifts "good managers." God gives us gifts. With those gifts comes the responsibility to manage them wisely. A lifestyle of stewardship includes the faithful, fruitful, daily management of the special gifts/talents you have received from God.

Why? Certainly to benefit men. But most important, to put your gifts into service to glorify God. Look what Peter says:

> *Are you a speaker? Speak as if you uttered the oracles of God! Do you give service? Give it as in the strength which God gives. In all things so act that the glory may be God's through Jesus Christ; to Him belong glory and power forever and ever. Amen.*
> — 1 Peter 4:11 NEB

Gifts are to use and share. Talent from God is not something to be hoarded. God's gifts are to be used to help people. They are not for bragging, but are for bringing the Good News to people.

Romans 12:6-8 exhorts Christians to use their gifts. Paul's partial list of gifts includes the gifts of prophecy, service, teaching, exhortation, giving, leadership, and mercy. These gifts, as well as other ministry gifts and offices listed in 1 Corinthians 12:28-31, are included in the "in all things" Peter mentions that are to be carried out, or acted upon, solely for God's glory.

Why do good stewards serve with their gifts? To glorify God.

Giving God glory means recognizing, reverencing, honoring, and praising Him for who He is — the One behind every good and perfect gift. James 1:17 says every good gift and perfect gift is from above, and cometh down from the Father of lights, with whom is no variableness, neither shadow of turning. God's gifts are good and perfect gifts.

> Christians are required, as servants and trustworthy stewards, to bring good to people and glory to God by faithfully using their God-given gifts.

As faithful servants of Christ and stewards of the mysteries of God, we are to do everything to the glory of God.

> *Whether then, you eat or drink or whatever you do, do all to the glory of God.*
> — 1 Corinthians 10:31

Christians are required, as servants and trustworthy stewards, to bring good to people and glory to God by faithfully using their God-given gifts.

## Glory Check

In light of 1 Corinthians 10:31, why do you serve? For what purpose or end do you serve God and people? Do you serve to glorify yourself, men or God?

_____

_____

_____

_____

_____

What does it mean to you to glorify God?

_____

_____

_____

_____

_____

List any areas of life where you need to do better in living for the glory of God.

_____

_____

_____

_____

In what practical ways can you improve your service to people and bring greater glory to God?

_____

_____

_____

## MAKE A COMMITMENT

I will begin this week to glorify God through the following behavior.

1. _____

2. _____

3. _____

4. _____

5. _____

# Managing Your Natural Talent

Throughout the basketball season, my wife and I have been privileged to watch many teams and players throughout our community. We have seen many talented young players, but one particular player in our city stood out on the court. Anyone and everyone in basketball circles was familiar with his name and game. His play was unmatched and was simply amazing! As a junior in high school, he was already being recruited by professional teams.

He possessed size, strength and coordination, exceptional ball-handling skills, uncanny court sense, and athletic finesse that guys like me can only dream of! This all-star athlete could dribble past any defender (or double team!), his shooting form was nearly flawless, and he appeared to glide through the air, effortlessly going to the basket to dunk the ball. How did he become so good at the game of basketball? Practice, hard work, and talent. He had outstanding natural athletic abilities.

> To become really good at anything, it takes practice, hard work, and talent.

Where did those athletic skills come from? His ability to play basketball was a God-given gift. God blessed this young man with exceptional natural athletic abilities. His Maker is the one who made this young man so able to play basketball. I rejoice that this exceptional athlete is also a fine young Christian. While being interviewed by a local sportscaster, he gave the Lord Jesus Christ the credit and glory for his abilities.

Natural talent. Some people are athletic, others artistic. Some can sing; others paint. Some people write, while others make money. Some decorate, while others plan and organize. Whether it is acting, dancing, speaking, writing, entertaining, administrating, running, catching a football, sewing a wedding dress, making straight "A's", or engineering a spaceship — people possess natural talent that comes from God.

> Natural talent is to be recognized, managed, and used for the glory of God. Stewardship of your natural gifts means that you realize that you will give account to God for the use or misuse of those natural abilities.

Natural talent is to be recognized, managed, and used for the glory of God. Stewardship of your natural gifts means that you realize that you will give account to God for the use or misuse of those natural abilities. As a Christian, you are required to faithfully manage all of God's resources, including natural talent. God expects you to be found trustworthy with the talent God has given you. Your life and the lives of others prosper when you are proven to be a good steward of your natural talent.

1.  What natural talents do you possess? What natural gifts make you stand out from others?

    _____

    _____

    _____

    _____

2.  Other people say that you are naturally gifted in these areas:

    _____

    _____

    _____

    _____

3.  What are you currently doing with your natural talents? Where are you using them? How are you improving them?

    _____

    _____

    _____

4. Who is benefiting from your natural gifts? In what way?

_____

_____

_____

_____

5. Are you using your natural talent to bring glory to God?

_____

_____

_____

6. How do you plan to use your natural gifts more for God's glory and the benefit of people around you?

_____

_____

_____

# Taking Care of the Body

Our natural and spiritual talents are housed within our physical bodies. In 2 Corinthians 5:1, Paul describes the physical body as the earthly tent which is our house. Our body is described as a "tent" or "house," a dwelling place where our soul and spirit are housed. This body we possess is a temporal tent that will one day give way to an eternal dwelling. (See 2 Corinthians 5:2-4.) Our "tent" or body is very important; we cannot express talent without a body.

Even though our earthly tent is temporal and subject to decay, it is God's will for us to live long, prosperous, satisfying lives. The Bible tells us God says in Psalm 91:16: "With a long life will I satisfy him...." Long life is God's preference for us. We live that long life out in a physical body. (Also see Genesis 15:15; Deuteronomy 5:23, 11:21; 1 Kings 3:14; Job 5:2; Proverbs 9:11, 10:2; Isaiah 65:22; Zechariah 8:4; and 1 Peter 3:10 regarding longevity.)

Long life and obedience are tied together. Solomon tells his son, in Proverbs 3:1-2, that there are benefits to keeping God's Word. One of benefit is long life: My son, do not forget my teaching, but let your heart keep my commandments; for length of days and years of life, and peace they will add to you.

*Even though our earthly tent is temporal and subject to decay, it is God's Will for us to live long, prosperous, satisfying lives.*

So, God gives length of days and years of life and peace to people who keep His commandments. Those are promises of prosperity or benefits of the righteous! What are some of the specific benefits of a long life versus a short life? Here are just a few: fulfill dreams; accomplish calling in life; develop potential; acquire wisdom; enjoy marriage and family life; greater influence for the Kingdom of God; leave a greater legacy; larger inheritance.

Long life is certainly preferable to one that is cut short for any reason.

But people can't live long lives and prosper if they are not healthy. Faithful stewardship of the body is vital to success in life. Your body is another gift from God that is entrusted to your care. Managing your physical health is a key component of lifestyle stewardship.

Sometimes we neglect out physical "tent." We take our health and vitality for granted, thinking that our bodies can take care of themselves. That is not true. Just sit around, neglect your body, and see what happens!

We must be active in managing our bodies if they are to be healthy and useful for God's purposes.

Study 1 Corinthians 6:12-20 very carefully. Paul shows believers what their physical body is and is not to be used for. In verse 13 Paul writes that the body is not for immorality, but for the Lord; and the Lord is for the body.

What four profound comments about your physical body does Paul make in verses 19-20? (See 1 Corinthians 3:16 and 2 Corinthians 6:16).

Your body is_____

Your body is_____

You (your body, soul, and spirit)_____

You are to_____in your body.

According to the context and content of this passage, to whom does your physical body belong? _____. Whose glory is your body to be used for, your own, or His? _____.

Clearly, the body is the Lord's. It is to be used for His glory!

As a holy temple belonging to God, your physical body will glorify Him when you keep it healthy and productive. It is your job and responsibility to manage your physical health and well being. That's what good stewards do!

We must be active in managing our bodies if they are to be healthy and useful for God's purposes.

# Helpful Hints for a Healthy Body

The following suggestions are lifestyle tips for maintaining a healthy body.

1. Keep up with regular physical examinations recommended by your physician. You must know the state of your body to manage it well.
2. Eat a well-balanced nutritious diet on a daily basis. Consult with a qualified nutritionist or dietitian. Choose a plan and stick with it.
3. Exercise aerobically regularly. A minimum of three times a week for at least thirty minutes. Get your heart pumping and your lungs breathing vigorously. Select type of workout that fits your personality type and personal preferences.
4. Adopt a "moderation" principle when exerting your body. Work and play hard, but avoid extremes whenever possible.
5. Avoid fad diets and weight reducing plans. Proper nutrition, regular aerobic exercise and self-discipline as a way of life over a lifetime will keep you healthy.
6. Abstain from addictive and harmful substances like alcohol, tobacco, and non-prescription, illegal drugs.
7. Pray over your body to be strong and healthy. Stand on God's promises of healing, health, and well-being in Jesus' name.

# Stewardship of Spiritual Gifts

We discovered earlier in this lesson that we have been given both natural and spiritual gifts. The spiritual gifts that we have received (listed in 1 Peter 4:11, Romans 12:3-8, 1 Corinthians 12:4-10, 28-31) are to be used in serving others. As we properly and faithfully manage these gifts through our service to others, we bring glory to God. We are to be found faithful, or trustworthy, as stewards of our spiritual gifts.

Spiritual gifts, like natural gifts, are useless if we don't use them. For the body of Christ, and in particular, the local church, to be effective in its witness, believers must be faithful in exercising their spiritual gifts. Without spiritual gifts, the body does not function properly and biblical fruit is not produced. The following steps will assist believers in putting their spiritual gifts to work for God.

## 1. Discover Your Gifts

Read the passages about spiritual gifts. Pray about your gifts. Ask the Holy Spirit to show you your specific gift or gift mix. Consult with your pastor or

> Spiritual gifts, like natural gifts, are useless if we don't use them. For the body of Christ, and in particular, the local church, to be effective in its witness, believers must be faithful in exercising their spiritual gifts.

spiritual elders. Ask them what gifts they see operating in you. Take a spiritual gift test. Confirm with your closest Christian friends the gifts they see in you. Focus in on the gift/s God has appointed for you.

## 2. Develop Your Gifts

Study scriptural examples of men and women who exercised your gifts. Read Christian books on spiritual gifts. Attend seminars about spiritual gifts. Spend time with Christians who have your similar gift. Learn from observation how their gifts are manifested.

## 3. Deploy Your Gifts

Volunteer for ministry positions where you can exercise your gifts. Seek every opportunity to use them. Get hands-on experience exercising your gifts. Make yourself available to those who can profit from them. Work hard at maturing your gift.

## 4. Duplicate Your Gifts

Mentor others in the body of Christ who have spiritual gifts similar to yours. Reproduce your ministry through others. Help them discover, develop, and deploy their gifts.

Evaluate yourself by answering the following questions.

1.  Have you discovered your spiritual gift/s? If so, list them.

    _____

    _____

    _____

    _____

    _____

    _____

    _____

    _____

    _____

2.  Are you developing your spiritual gift/s? If so, how?

    _____

    _____

    _____

    _____

    _____

    _____

Confirm with your closest Christian friends the gifts they see in you. Focus in on the gift(s) God has appointed for you.

3. Have you deployed your spiritual gift/s? If so, where?

_____

_____

_____

4. Have you duplicated your spiritual gift/s? If so, in whom?

_____

_____

_____

# Excel at What You Do Well

This entire lesson has been devoted to managing your talent. There is only one proven pathway to faithfully using your natural/spiritual talents for the glory of God and the good of others. It's called excellence. What God has gifted you to do, do it well. Excel at what you do well!

> *This I pray, that your love may abound still more and more in real knowledge and all discernment, so that you approve the things that are excellent, in order to be sincere and blameless until the day of Christ; having been filled with the fruit of righteousness which comes through Jesus Christ, to the glory and praise of God.*
> — Philippians 1:9-11

What God has gifted you to do, do it well. Excel at what you do well!

# Lesson 11

## Managing Your Treasure — PART I

*Honor the Lord from your wealth, and from the first of all your produce. So your barns will be filled with plenty, and your vats will overflow with new wine.*
— Proverbs 3:9-10

*"Bring the whole tithe into the storehouse, so that there may be food in My house, and test Me now in this," says the Lord of hosts, "if I will not open for you the windows of heaven, and pour out for you a blessing until it overflows."*
— Malachi 3:10

### PRINCIPLE

- Financial prosperity and blessing are promised to those who manage their money according to God's plan.

### PURPOSE

God entrusts money and material resources to our care. He richly blesses those who take seriously their responsibility to be trustworthy stewards of their God-given resources.

Our purpose in this lesson is two-fold. First, we will learn how God promises to prosper people who manage their money according to the proven principles found in His Word. Second, we will layout a scriptural, step-by-step plan that is practical, profitable, and attainable.

Strategy always precedes success. Unfortunately, many Christians fail in financial stewardship because they fail to follow God's prescribed plan for prosperity. Mature Christians, on the other hand, understand the importance of managing their God-given treasure in a manner that honors God and helps meet the needs of men. They willingly and gladly implement the Bible's plan for personal and corporate financial/material prosperity.

### DISCUSSION

Stewardship of finances shows who in the Kingdom of God has strength, courage, and loyalty and who does not. Regarding stewardship, more professing

Strategy always precedes success. Unfortunately, many Christians fail in financial stewardship because they fail to follow God's prescribed plan for prosperity.

Christians stumble in this area of managing their money and resources than any other area. Too many possess the attitude of the congregation in the following story.

> An evangelist preaching to a congregation told the people, "This church, like the crippled man, has got to get up and walk!"
> And the people said, "That's right! Let it walk."
> "This church," he continued, "like Elijah on Mount Carmel, has got to run!"
> "Let it run, preacher!" they agreed.
> "This church has got to mount up on wings like eagles and fly!" he cried.
> They responded, "Let it fly!"
> "If it flies, it takes money!" he shouted.
> And they shouted, "Let it walk!"

When it comes to financial giving, many Christians show their support in words, but not action. Believers know it takes finances to reach people for Christ, but few actually participate in giving. In many Christian settings, when you talk about money some people get defensive, almost defiant. They're offended when pastors preach about giving money to God's work. That's terribly shortsighted.

People not only hinder God's work for others, they hurt themselves when they balk at financial stewardship. If they would open their hearts and minds to God's Word, they would see that He has established a great plan for their financial prosperity and economic well being.

God wants us to prosper! He has even shown us in His Word the exact steps necessary to successfully manage our money. There's no guesswork at all. We simply follow the steps and are blessed. All we must do is prove ourselves trustworthy through faith and obedience.

## Money...Blessing or Curse?

Money plays an important role in our everyday lives. Not a single day goes by that we don't have to deal with finances in some way. We must purchase necessities, pay bills, manage a household, run a business, provide governmental and institutional services for people. Money is necessary for spreading the Gospel. Money, money, money. Managing finances is an inescapable fact of life.

Money can be a blessing or a curse, a tool that can be used for great good or great evil. Jesus spent a tremendous amount of His time teaching about money

God wants us to prosper! He has even shown us in His Word the exact steps necessary to successfully manage our money. There's no guesswork at all.

and its proper use. In fact, there are more scriptures on the subject of money, finances, and stewardship than on the subjects of heaven and hell! Check your concordance. If Jesus focused on finances that much, money management must be important to God.

As in all other areas of stewardship, we will give an account to God for the use of our finances and material resources. As the servants and stewards in Luke 16:1-13 and Luke 19:11-27 were accountable to their masters, so we are accountable to our Lord and Master.

Faithful money management springs from the heart. When it comes to managing our treasure, our heart determines our behavior. We manage money according to the way we perceive the purpose of money. A biblical attitude that is Christ-like in nature is critical to successful stewardship of our material resources.

> When it comes to managing our treasure, our heart determines our behavior.

Before we present a proven strategy for successful stewardship of money, let's consider different types of givers and money managers found in God's Word.

## Three Types of Financial Givers

> *Remember this: he who sows sparingly and grudgingly will also reap sparingly and grudgingly, and he who sows generously, that blessings may come to someone, will also reap generously and with blessings. Let each one give as he has made up his own mind and purposed in his heart not reluctantly or sorrowfully or under compulsion, for God loves, He takes pleasure in, prizes above other things, and is unwilling to abandon or to do without, a cheerful, joyous, prompt to do it giver whose heart is in his giving.*
> — 2 Corinthians 9:6-7 AMP

In Eleanor Doan's *Speaker's Sourcebook*, we find an illustration of three kinds of givers: the flint, the sponge, and the honeycomb. To get anything from a flint you must hammer it; then you get only chips and sparks. To get water from a sponge, you must squeeze it; the more pressure, the more water. But the honeycomb just overflows with its own sweetness.

The Apostle Paul, in the above passage, also addresses three types of givers found in the body of Christ. They all give, but they bring their gifts to God in very different ways. Notice that Paul says in verse seven, that "each one" gives in the way they give because they have purposed in their heart and made up their own minds to do so. You determine the kind of giver you are!

Paul describes sad, mad, and glad givers.

## Sad givers

These persons give "sorrowfully." They mourn when they let go of their money. Their faces fall when the offering plate passes by. These givers are sad because they interpret giving as loss. "Parting is such sweet sorrow" could be their motto for giving money. Their personal philosophy of giving is based on what they perceive they have to give up, not what they can give to.

They are the sponges. Sad givers must be squeezed in order to get anything out of them. Sad givers are bereaved and grieved regarding opportunity to give.

Have you ever seen a sad giver? What did they look like? What did they say about giving? Did you like their attitude?

_____

_____

_____

_____

How have you ever been a sad giver? Be honest now.

_____

_____

_____

_____

Why were you sad about giving money to God?

_____

_____

_____

Why was it so hard for you to part with your money?

_____

_____

_____

_____

What do you think God thinks about sad giving?

_____

_____

_____

Being sad and sorrowful is a sad way to give and live.

> Sad givers must be squeezed in order to get anything out of them. Sad givers are bereaved and grieved regarding opportunity to give.

## Mad Givers

They give to relieve pressure. They give grudgingly because they feel they have to. They are the flint. Lots of sparks fly when they give. They don't give because they want to, they give out of a sense of obligation and duty, not delight. They may let their money go, but they are upset about it, and because they are grumpy about it, others sense their displeasure.

Mad givers experience a titanic, emotional tug of war in their hearts when it comes to giving their finances. They don't grieve; they get angry! They question why they have to give. Selfish to the core, their attitude blinds them to looking at life as a wonderful opportunity to do good through giving.

Mad givers are hateful and spiteful towards the opportunity to give.

Describe what you think a mad giver looks and acts like.

_____

_____

_____

> Mad givers experience a titanic, emotional tug-of-war in their hearts when it comes to giving their finances. They don't grieve; they get angry!

Were you ever mad when you gave something to God?

_____

_____

_____

How did it feel inside feeling angry about giving?

_____

_____

_____

What does a mad giver need to do to change his attitude toward giving?

_____

_____

_____

Being mad leads to high blood pressure and lost opportunities to do lasting good to others with a sweet spirit.

## Glad Givers

This type of giver is always sweet, never sad, sour or bitter. Joy marks the glad giver's style. They give cheerfully, not tearfully like the sad givers, or fearfully like the mad givers. Glad givers don't have to give — they get to give! They give because they want to, and they truly like to.

The word translated *cheerful* in this verse actually means "hilarious." Unrestrained joy and happiness flow from the heart of Glad givers when they have opportunity to give. They can't wait to give. Other people easily sense their excitement. Glad givers make things happen in God's Kingdom.

To Glad givers, giving is gain. They never need coaxing or convincing. When approached about giving opportunities, they are the first to give. Deep joy in their hearts motivates them to give cheerfully. They are the sweet honeycombs. Because they purpose in their hearts to be cheerful, this type of giver oozes and overflows with joy and happiness. They're fun to be around.

Glad givers are grateful for the opportunity to give. It's a happy event for them. According to the Apostle, which giver does God love? The Glad, or cheerful giver of course! God takes great delight in, prizes above the others, the person who is cheerful and joyful about giving. Make no mistake about it. God loves to receive gifts from Glad givers.

Do you personally know any Glad givers? What do you like about them?

_____

_____

_____

Are you a Glad giver? If so, why? What makes you happy about giving?

_____

_____

_____

How would you describe glad giving to someone?

_____

_____

Why do you think God loves the "cheerful" giver?

_____

_____

_____

_____

Glad giving is the only way to give in God's Kingdom!

Glad givers are grateful for the opportunity to give. It's a happy event for them.

According to the Apostle, which giver does God love? The Glad, or cheerful giver of course!

Faithful managers of God's money are Glad givers. They love to give of their finances. They can be counted on to give consistently and cheerfully. They joyfully adopt the following plan, (which is found in the Bible) for prosperity.

# Whose Money Is It, Anyway?

Your money is not your money. It is God's. Remember: He owns the cattle (That includes the cash too!) and we manage the ranch. Our Maker entrusts us to manage money and material resources wisely and according to biblical principles.

Proverbs 3:9 commands us: Honor the Lord from your wealth, and from the first of all your produce. The person who would be prosperous and useful in life shows honor to (recognizes, treats with deference and respect) the Lord through the wise use of his wealth and material resources. Successful stewards show respect to God by managing their money well. They recognize the fact that their money has come from God as a trust. There is a spiritual principle here that governs the lifestyle of successful stewards.

> Your money is not your money. It is God's. Remember: He owns the cattle (That includes the cash too!) and we manage the ranch.

The principle: Honor the Lord with your wealth and He will honor you with plenty and prosperity.

Read Proverbs 3:10. What does it say happens to those who honor the Lord with their wealth?

_____

_____

_____

_____

Those who honor God with their wealth (money) and the first portion of all their produce (material resources) are blessed with prosperity. "First portion" means that God is first priority. He gets the first part, the prime piece and parcel of the produce, never the leftovers or the last part.

Note the words *plenty* and *overflow*. Those are words of blessing. Those who manage their treasure in a way that honors the Lord will have barns (a picture of a farm/home) that are bursting with plenty of goods. Their families are well provided for. Their vats (which represents business enterprise) will be spilling over with not old, but new wine. Their businesses increase and prosper. What a great picture of blessing and benefit for those who put God first in finances.

God honors and provides prosperity to people who honor Him with their wealth.

Those who "honor God with their wealth" adopt and follow a scriptural strategy, or biblical game plan for successful management of their money and material resources.

God honors and provides prosperity to people who honor Him with their wealth.

# Scriptural Strategy for Successful Money Management

God's plan for success in financial stewardship includes tithes, offerings, alms (benevolent giving to the poor and needy), debt management, savings and investments, life insurance, legal wills, inheritances, and proper care of material assets.

## The Tithe: God's Foundation for Financial Success
Take your Bible and read the following Scriptures on tithing.

| | | |
|---|---|---|
| Genesis 14:20 | Leviticus 27:30-32 | Deuteronomy 12:17 |
| Deuteronomy 14:22-28 | Nehemiah 10:28-38 | 2 Chronicles 31:5-12 |
| Deuteronomy 26:12 | Nehemiah 13:12 | Malachi 3:7-12 |
| Nehemiah 12:44 | Luke 11:42 | Luke 18:12 |
| Hebrews 7:1-10 | Matthew 23:23 | |

Summarize from your personal study what God's Word say about tithing.

_____

_____

_____

_____

_____

_____

# Biblical Truths About Tithing

## The Tithe Is Holy
First and foremost, the Bible says the tithe is holy. To be holy means to be "set apart for sacred purposes." If you study the word *holy* throughout Scripture, you will find that holy things are not common things. They are very special. Holy items (locations, altars, land, buildings, utensils, people, the tithe, etc.) are set aside for God and His use.

Leviticus 27:30 says all the tithe of the land, of the seed of the land or of the fruit of the tree, it is the Lord's; it is holy to the Lord. Note the tithe is holy and it is holy unto the Lord. It is not to be taken lightly. We must be very careful how we use that which God designates as holy. Holy things must be used in the way the Holy One has appointed for them to be used. They are never to be touched or used in an unholy manner.

## The Tithe Belongs to God

The tithe is not man's. "It is the Lord's," as we saw in Leviticus 27:30. We have no right to it because it belongs to the Lord; it is His property, not ours. The tithe, in the Old and New Testaments was always given to God, never to man.

God has every right to the tithe because it belongs to Him. Since the "tithe is the Lord's," what right have we to withhold it? What right have we to borrow it? What right have we to divert it? What right have we to use it at all?

In His wisdom, God promises to bless those who release the tithe to Him because they recognize that it is the Lord's, not theirs.

## The Tithe Is Commanded by God

Tithing is not a suggestion. It is a "thou shalt." Deuteronomy 12:22 declares: "Thou shalt truly tithe...." (KJV) and "You shall surely tithe" (NAS). Tithing is the law of God. Laws are made for the common good, and are expected to be obeyed.

If there were no other reason for tithing, that fact that it is God's law is reason enough. Tithing is biblically based. The principle was established in the Old Testament and its practice is endorsed in the New.

Tithing is a law of God that has gone unaltered for centuries. Malachi did not repeal tithing; he amplified it (Malachi 3:7-12). Jesus did not repeal it; he commended it (Matthew 23:23). The writer to the Hebrews did not repeal tithing; he reaffirmed it (Hebrews 7:4-8). The early church did not repeal it; they practiced it. Tithing has stood the test of time as a commandment from the Lord.

## The Tithe Is the First Tenth of Our Income

The word *tithe* means " a tenth," or ten percent. Biblically, God's tithe is not a tenth, but "the tenth." Genesis 28:10-22 gives us the record of Jacob's dream at a place he called Bethel. He made a vow there, and part of his pledge was to pay the tithe on whatever God gave to Him. Verse 22 says, *"This stone, which I have set up as a pillar, will be God's house; and of all that Thou dost give me I will surely give the tenth to Thee."* (KJV)

God has every right to the tithe because it belongs to Him. Since the "tithe is the Lord's," what right have we to withhold it? What right have we to borrow it? What right have we to divert it? What right have we to use it at all?

In the Word of God, "the tenth" means the first tenth. God's people were always directed to bring the first part of their produce to the Lord. They always set apart their firstborn sons to God. Firstfruits is a common biblical phrase. First is right because of who God is and what He has done for us. God, who is so good to us, is to have first place in a believer's life. Therefore, He should be given the firstfruits of our finances.

The tithe that is holy and belongs to the Lord is the first tenth of our total income. Not the middle, or last ten percent, but the very first.

## The Tithe is the Minimum, Not the Maximum

The first ten percent of our income is the beginning point of biblical stewardship. The tithe is the baseline. Faithful management of money builds upon the tithe.

The tithe provides a solid foundation for offerings and other types of financial giving. Malachi 3:8 speaks of "tithes and offerings." If the tithe were all that God required of us, there would be no need to mention offerings here and in many other places in the Bible. The tithe is the beginning, the starting point of financial stewardship, not the end or finish.

## Tithing Is a Matter of Obedience

Commands are given to be obeyed. God always blesses obedience. Tithing is never an issue of opinion or convenience. Tithing boils down to obedience. Withholding the tithe is disobedience. Giving the tithe is being obedient. Paying the tithe is not optional if we want to be obedient to the Lord.

## Tithing Is a Trust

Tithing is the cornerstone of stewardship. When we tithe, we take God as our partner, and He takes us as His partner. Tithing is a matter of trust. Trust between partners. He trusts us to trust Him and His Word. We trust His Word and trust Him to keep His promises of blessing to those who trust Him with the tithe. Faithful stewards are to be found trustworthy (1 Corinthians 4:2) — this includes the matter of tithing. Tithing is a tangible demonstration of trust in God.

## Tithing Puts God to the Test

To tithe or not to tithe is the question we all must answer. Tithing is a critical test of true discipleship and faithful stewardship. It's a test of our faith and obedience. Tithing tests our dedication and devotion to God and His work.

But tithing also puts God to the test. How do we know that? He said so. In Malachi 3:10, God says "Test or prove Me in this…." Put Me to the test. I am

The tithe that is holy and belongs to the Lord is the first tenth of our total income. Not the middle, or last ten percent, but the very first.

ready to be examined. I have declared that I will bless you if you tithe. Test Me with your tithe. I will prove to you that My Word is good.

In the next lesson, we will see the abundant blessings God brings to those who bring the tithe to Him.


## TITHING QUESTIONS

What objections about the tithing principle have you heard from Christians who do not tithe?

_____

_____

_____

_____

_____

To tithe or not to tithe is the question we all must answer. Tithing is a critical test of true discipleship and faithful stewardship.

Is the devil for or against tithing? If he were against tithing, why would Satan oppose tithers?

_____

_____

_____

_____

_____

If you are not a tither, why have you chosen not to tithe?

_____

_____

_____

_____

Do you have a biblical basis for being a non-tither?

_____

_____

_____

_____

_____

_____

_____

# Lesson 12

## Managing Your Treasure — PART II

*"From the days of your fathers you have turned aside from My statutes, and have not kept them. Return to Me, and I will return to you," says the Lord of hosts. "But you say, 'How shall we return?' Will a man rob God? Yet you are robbing Me! But you say, 'How have we robbed Thee?' In tithes and offerings. You are cursed with a curse, for you are robbing Me, the whole nation of you! Bring the whole tithe into the storehouse, so that there may be food in My house, and test Me now in this," says the Lord of hosts, "If I will not open for you the windows of heaven, and pour out for you a blessing until it overflows. Then I will rebuke the devourer for you, so that it may not destroy the fruits of the ground; nor will your vine in the field cast its grapes," says the Lord of hosts. "And all the nations will call you blessed, for you shall be a delightful land," says the Lord of hosts.*
— Malachi 3:7-12

### PRINCIPLE
- Faithfulness in finances is a mark of Christian maturity.

## Bring the Tithe to the Storehouse and Be Blessed!

Faithfulness in finances is a mark of Christian maturity.

Let's take a detailed look at this most familiar passage on tithing in the Bible. The teaching on tithing contains three main points: an accusation, an invitation, and a proclamation.

### God's Accusation (verses 7-9)
Why was God upset with His children Israel?

_____

_____

_____

What did He accuse them of?

_____

_____

What was the penalty for their transgressions?

_____

_____

_____

Israel had strayed from God by not obeying His statutes. They were out of favor with Him and were not receiving His blessing. God said that in order to return to God's favor and good graces, they had to stop stealing from Him. That's right! He said His people were robbing Him.

How is it possible for humans to steal from Almighty God? By withholding their tithes and offerings. People rob God when they refuse to tithe.

God accused Israel of robbing Him. He said they were taking what rightfully belonged to Him. By keeping the tithe, they brought upon themselves a curse. The whole nation was being disobedient. Because of their disobedience to the commandment to tithe, the whole nation of Israel was "cursed with a curse." They knew better — but they chose to forfeit God's blessing by stealing the tithe from Him.

### God's Invitation (vv. 7, 10)

Though Israel had been disobedient, what did God invite them to do (v. 7)?

_____

_____

_____

_____

_____

What were they to bring into the storehouse? (v. 10)

_____

_____

_____

_____

_____

Why were they to bring "the whole tithe" to God?

_____

_____

_____

_____

_____

> How is it possible for humans to steal from Almighty God? By withholding their tithes and offerings. People rob God when they refuse to tithe.

Even though Israel had disobeyed Him, God loved Israel. He issued an invitation for them to return to Him. If they would return to Him, He would return to them. Fellowship and partnership would be restored.

Israel asked how they might return to God. God gave His people very specific directions as to how to come back to Him. His directions were unmistakably clear. Start obeying Me. Begin by bringing the whole tithe to My storehouse. Stop stealing the tithe and offerings from Me. Bring them so there will be food in My house.

## UNDERSTANDING THREE THINGS WAS KEY TO ISRAEL'S RETURNING TO THE LORD

### Bring

The first act is to bring the whole tithe to God. Bringing is our part. God never does the bringing for us. Bring is an action verb. It requires us getting up and doing something. Get up, get out, and deliver your tithe check (the first full ten percent of your income) to the Lord. Israel was to bring their tithes and offerings to the Lord, not cling to them and withhold them from Him. Bringing brings blessing.

### The Whole Tithe

Bring the entire tithe, not part of it. There are people who call themselves tithers, but they actually only give 1, or 2, or 5, or 7 percent of their income to the Lord. These people are giving regularly, but they are not tithing. A tithe is not a tithe until it is a full ten percent! We aren't tithing unless we are giving the top ten percent of our income to God.

God made it plain to Israel: Bring the whole tithe, then the curse will lift and I will bless you!

We can't expect God's fullest blessing when we are only willing to do part of what He asks!

### Storehouse

In the Old Testament, God's storehouse (note "food in My house") was the Tabernacle, and later, the Temple. The official gathering places, where the people worshipped God and received teaching and ministry from His Word, were the storehouse. In the New Testament, the storehouse became the local church fellowship. Under the supervision of the apostles, tithes and offerings were received in the home fellowships, synagogue settings, and the first church buildings.

"The whole tithe" is to be paid (brought) where a person receives teaching and ministry. Today, the storehouse for the tithe is the local church, the spiritual home of the believer. Special gifts and offerings over and above the tithe can

Israel was to bring their tithes and offerings to the Lord, not cling to them and withhold them from Him. Bringing brings blessing.

go to other ministries, but "the whole tithe" belongs in the local congregation where a Christian is a member.

Tithing provides "food" for the local church so it can carry out its mission and minister to its community.

### God's Proclamation (vv. 10-12)

What did God promise His people He would do if they brought their tithes to Him?

_____

_____

_____

_____

Who would God rebuke on their behalf?

_____

_____

_____

_____

Israel would then be called what by the other nations?

_____

_____

_____

_____

_____

Tithing opens heaven's windows. A window is an opening, a channel. Windows (plural) means multiple openings and channels.

In a nutshell, God says, You bring the tithe, and watch me bless your lives. Prove Me if I will not open the windows of heaven (note the plural form of window) and pour out blessings so bountiful that they will overflow and you will have a hard time containing them. (Again a picture of plenty and abundance — prosperity.)

If Israel would bring the tithe in, God would pour the blessing on. Tithing opens heaven's windows. A window is an opening, a channel. Windows (plural) means multiple openings and channels. Supernaturally and naturally, God blesses His tithers through all kinds of income streams. God is not limited in any way in being creative in getting financial blessings to His children. Heaven's channels of richest blessings are closed to non-tithers, but wide open to those who faithfully bring the whole tithe unto God's storehouse.

Tithers also receive another important financial benefit. God rebukes the devourer for them. They don't have to battle the enemy who tries to steal their prosperity. God fights on their behalf.

The tithe guarantees that God will keep the devourer far from you, your household, your money, and your material resources. It's great knowing that God is guarding your stuff because you are a tither.

If you think you can't afford to tithe, think again. In light of God's promises to tithers, you can't afford not to tithe!

## SUMMARY

Tithing is a significant sign of the Lordship of Jesus Christ in our lives. It has been truly said, "If Jesus is not Lord of all, He is not Lord at all." If we do not tithe, Jesus is not Lord of our money. If He is not Lord of our money, which plays such a significant part in our daily living, how can He be Lord of our lives?

In reality, robbing God of tithes and offerings is robbing ourselves. God has pledged Himself to bless tithers. If we choose not to tithe, we steal from God and rob Him of the opportunity to bless our lives. We cut off God's promises of prosperity when we refuse to tithe.

Here's the good news! God loves to prove His promises. He always passes His part of the tithing test. The question is: Will we pass our part? We can choose to tithe.

*If you think you can't afford to tithe, think again. In light of God's promises to tithers, you can't afford not to tithe!*

# Offerings — Over and Above the Tithe

An offering is something given in worship of God, and to support the work of the church. Offerings of various kinds were given throughout Scripture. There were burnt offerings (Exodus 29:18), drink offerings (Exodus 29:40), sheave offerings (Exodus 29:27), meal or meat offerings (Leviticus 2:1), peace offerings (Exodus 29:24), sin offerings (Exodus 29:14), thank offerings (Leviticus 7:12,) and monetary offerings or collections (1 Corinthians 16:2). Each type of offering served a specific purpose, but in general, offerings were given to the Lord as an act of worship, giving praise, an act of thanksgiving, or for meeting the needs of others.

In 1 Corinthians 16:2, Paul instructed the Christians at Corinth concerning a special collection or offering that was being taken to bring relief to fellow Christians who were experiencing a time of distress.

> *Now concerning the collection for the saints, as I directed the churches of Galatia, so do you also. On the first day of every week let each one of you put aside and save, as he may prosper, that no collections be made when I come.*
> — 1 Corinthians 16:2

Paul was receiving offerings from various churches. The believers were instructed to put aside money as God had prospered them. They were to save this offering until the proper time for collection (which was the day of worship). When Paul arrived, the collection was to have already been taken. This collection, or offering, was not the tithe. It was over and above the tithe.

We learned earlier from Malachi 3:7 that God rebuked Israel for robbing Him of both "tithes and offerings." Not only were the people withholding the first ten percent, they weren't giving Him anything else either. "Tithes and offerings" both belonged to God. If the people desired to turn a curse into a blessing, they had to obey the Lord's instruction to bring the whole tithe to Him first.

We give the tithe out of obedience. It is the minimum obligation that satisfies what is due to God. It is our rent for the space we occupy and the resources we use. The tithe declares we are obeying God.

On the other hand, offerings are gifts of love. "Giving" actually begins when we give offerings. Whereas the tithe is our duty, offerings are our delight. We give above the tithe because of our gratitude for God's goodness in our lives. Offerings are a statement that we love God.

Offerings are also seed that we sow into the Kingdom of God. The earth's processes and God's economic system operate according to the principle of seedtime and harvest. Genesis 8:22 states that while the earth remains, seedtime and harvest, and cold and heat, and summer and winter, and day and night, shall not cease. Just as night follows day and winter follows summer, harvest always follows seed sowing. Seedtime and harvest. It's a law of life.

According to 2 Corinthians 9, sowing financial seed reaps financial harvest. When we give offerings (sow seed), there is always a blessing (harvest). When we sow seed with our offerings, God meets our needs and the needs of others. How much

*Offerings are also seed that we sow into the Kingdom of God. The earth's processes and God's economic system operate according to the principle of seedtime and harvest.*

we reap in financial blessing depends on how much we sow. (See 2 Corinthians 9:6.) Study 2 Corinthians 9:10-13 and answer the following questions.)

1. Who supplies seed to the sower and then multiplies the sower's seed?

   _____

   _____

   _____

   _____

   _____

2. Who is enriched because of their liberality in seed sowing?

   _____

   _____

   _____

   _____

   _____

3. Who receives thanksgiving when Christians sow seed through offerings?

   _____

   _____

   _____

   _____

   _____

   _____

4. Whose needs were fully supplied?

   _____

   _____

   _____

   _____

   _____

Scripture sets no percentage for an offering. The amount of an offering is guided by two primary principles: as we purpose in our heart (See 2 Corinthians 9:7,) and according to our ability (See 2 Corinthians 8:12 and 1 Corinthians 16:2.) The first step to faithful stewardship of finances is to tithe. The second step is to give offerings as the Spirit of God directs us.

The amount of an offering is guided by two primary principles: as we purpose in our heart (See 2 Corinthians 9:7,) and according to our ability (See 2 Corinthians 8:12 and 1 Corinthians 16:2.).

# Giving to the Less Fortunate (Alms-Giving)

Our money is not our own; it is not given to us just for our use. Almsgiving is a biblical principle, and practice that many modern-day Christians have overlooked. The word *alms* means an act of charity or benevolence. It has at its root a sense or spirit of pity and charity that takes deliberate action in giving something freely (money, food, clothing, etc.) to relieve the plight of the poor.

In your own words, what do the following Scriptures say concerning God's attitude and care for the poor? (1 Samuel 2:8; Job 36:6; Psalm 10:14, 35:10, 40:17, 70:5, 72:12, 74:21, 82:4, 86:1, 109.22; Ecclesiastes 5:8; Jeremiah 20:13; Luke 16:22).

_____

_____

_____

_____

_____

_____

Study Psalm 41:1, 82:3; Proverbs 14:21, 19:17, 21:13, 29:14; Jeremiah 22:16; Exodus 23:11; and Galatians 2:10. What should a Christian's attitude and conduct be toward the poor and needy?

_____

_____

_____

Old and New Testament scriptures heartily endorse the practice of almsgiving.

> *In case a countryman of yours becomes poor and his means with regard to you falter, then you are to sustain him (relieve him), like a stranger or a sojourner, that he may live with you.*
> — Leviticus 25:35

> *If there is a poor man with you, one of your brothers, in any of your towns in your land which the Lord your God is giving you, you shall not harden your heart, nor close your hand from your poor brother, but you shall freely open your hand to him, and generously lend (give) him sufficient for his need in whatever he lacks*
> — Deuteronomy 15:7-8

> The word *alms* means an act of charity or benevolence. It has at its root a sense or spirit of pity and charity that takes deliberate action in giving something freely (money, food, clothing, etc.) to relieve the plight of the poor.

*Jesus said to him [the rich young ruler], "If you want to be complete, go and sell your possessions and give to the poor, and you shall have treasure in heaven; and come follow Me.*
— *Matthew 19:21*

God prospers us so we can, as His stewards, meet the needs of needy people. Faithful management of monetary and material resources must include sharing what we have with the poor. We are to give alms according to the following principle and pattern found in the Word.

## Give Alms to the Poor from What You Possess

*Give alms of such things as you have; and, behold all things are clean unto you.*
— Luke 11:41 KJV

Benevolence is given according to what we have to give. If you have money, give money. If clothing, clothing. If food, food. If goods and services, goods and services. Everyone can be an almsgiver, because everyone has something to give.

Nowhere in Scripture are believers told to sell all they have and give it to the poor. Only one man (a non-believer in Christ) was told to do that.

Jesus instructed the rich young ruler to sell his possessions and give them to the poor. (See Matthew 19:16-26.) Why? Because the young man didn't own his possessions; they owned him. He was a slave to his stuff. His goods were his god. Jesus was teaching a lesson on successful stewardship, not declaring a doctrine of self-impoverishment for the sake of the poor.

The rich young ruler turned his back on Jesus' offer because his earthly riches were more important to him than heavenly riches. He failed the test of managing his treasure faithfully. He walked away from a once-in-a-lifetime opportunity to possess real riches and experience true greatness.

## Give Alms Privately, Not Publicly

*Take heed that you do not do your alms before men, to be seen of them; otherwise you have no reward of your Father who is in heaven. Therefore when thou doest thine alms, do not sound a trumpet before thee, as the hypocrites do in the synagogues and in the streets, that they may have glory of men. Verily I say unto you, they have their reward. But when thou doest alms, let not thy left hand know what thy right hand doeth; that thine alms may be in secret; and thy Father which seeth in secret himself shall reward thee openly.*
— Matthew 6:1-4

Benevolence is given according to what we have to give. If you have money, give money. If clothing, clothing. If food, food. If goods and services, goods and services. Everyone can be an almsgiver, because everyone has something to give.

Almsgiving is never to be a show. According to Jesus, we are to give privately and anonymously. No public fanfare. Don't even let your right hand know what your left hand is up to. Give gifts to people who can't give to you in return. Give your gifts anonymously through somebody else. The dignity and esteem of the needy person is preserved when we give in this manner. Our almsgiving is not to be seen by others. Shallow rewards come to those who parade their benevolence before people. God sees what we do in secret — and He richly rewards the person who is good to the poor and is not hypocritical about it.

Another key to managing your treasure is giving some of your money and material goods to the poor on a regular basis. There is no greater joy than relieving the needs of a poor person in the name of Jesus!

> Don't even let your right hand know what your left hand is up to. Give gifts to people who can't give to you in return. Give your gifts anonymously through somebody else.

## SEARCH YOUR HEART

Are the poor and needy included in your financial giving strategy?

_____
_____
_____
_____

Who do you know that is in need at this time?

_____
_____
_____
_____

What do you have to give them?

_____
_____
_____
_____

This is what I plan to give them and how I plan to get it to them.

_____
_____
_____
_____

# Managing Debt Successfully

Debt. That four-letter financial word that nobody likes. Excessive debt-loads, those that are unreasonable and unmanageable, are mortal enemies of anyone attempting to be a good and faithful steward of their God-given resources. Out-of-control debt destroys more financial portfolios than anything else.

Basically, debt occurs when people live beyond their means. Borrowing money and buying things on credit instead of paying for them with cash will create debt quickly. A word about credit cards. If your credit card is mastering you and making you a slave to debt, get rid of it.

It is not a sin to borrow. The Bible is not opposed to lending and borrowing money. Read Deuteronomy 28:12. This verse mentions both lending and borrowing. If it were a sin to borrow money, then those lending it would be sinning also. The point of Deuteronomy 28:12 is this: Lenders are more blessed than borrowers. We are blessed if we do not borrow, not because borrowing is wrong, but because lending puts us in position of strength while borrowing puts us in a position of weakness.

The lender has advantage over the borrower. Proverbs 22:7 says the rich rules over the poor, and the borrower becomes the lender's slave. In James 2:6 we read: "But you have dishonored the poor man. Is it not the rich who oppress you and personally drag you into court." When we are indebted to someone, we have signed over, and surrendered control of, our assets and resources. Someone else is in charge regarding our money.

Sometimes debt is necessary. Purchasing a home, college education, and big-ticket items can require substantial outlays of cash upfront that we do not possess ourselves. But if we borrow, our debt should be reasonable, manageable, and paid off as soon as possible.

If you want to manage debt successfully, live within your income level, strive to live debt free as much as possible, and make it your long-term goal to be financially independent.

When God's people are in debt to the world, the wealth of the righteous goes to the wicked, rather than the wealth of the wicked coming to the righteous.

> If you want to manage debt successfully, live within your income level, strive to live debt free as much as possible, and make it your long-term goal to be financially independent.

# Prospering Through Savings and Investments

For years, in premarital counseling I have advised couples to establish their financial house on three initial payment principles: pay your tithes; pay your taxes; and pay yourself through savings and investments. This ensures that God, the government, and your household will be taken care of.

Scripture supports all three payments. God and the tithe (Malachi 3:7-12), government and taxes (Matthew 22:15-22, 17:24-27; Mark 12:13-16; and Romans 13:6), and personal savings (Deuteronomy 28:5 and Proverbs 21:20).

Read and reflect on these scriptures regarding personal savings.

> *Blessed shall be your basket* ("store" in KJV) *and kneading bowl.*
> — Deuteronomy 28:5

> *In the house of the wise are stores of choice food and oil, but fools spend whatever they get.*
> — Proverbs 21:20 NIV

> *The wise have wealth and luxury, but a foolish man devours all he has.*
> — Proverbs 21:20 TLB

To save something means to put it back or set it aside. In the Old Testament, the word *store* was used to mean the place where goods and money were put back or saved.

Everyone needs a store, or saving place. According to Proverbs 21:20, wise people save some of what they possess; foolish men spend all they have. Wisdom dictates that instead of consuming everything immediately, we should be smart, save something, and put it back for tomorrow.

Deuteronomy 28:5 declares that for the person who obeys God, their store, or their saving place, will be blessed. Conversely, Deuteronomy 28:17 says one of the consequences for the one who chooses to disobey God is that his store will be cursed. Note that whether blessed or cursed, both persons have a store. A savings account can't be blessed if a person doesn't have one!

Savings provide a hedge, a buffer, against unforeseen financial needs. They are something to fall back on if necessary. Savings are an asset, a tangible resource. They are also a source of money that can provide leverage when being considered for acquiring even more money. Saving money is always a plus.

People with savings have an advantage over those who don't. It's a financial fact: Saving money and building a nest egg will hatch prosperity.

## Simple Savings Plan

1. You can't save money if you don't have a place to save it! Open a savings account. Don't put your savings in a sock under your mattress.
2. Save something. Start with a small amount. Saving something is always preferable to saving nothing! Start small, then think big!
3. Contribute regularly. A little bit over a long time becomes a lot. Money accumulating interest over time is to your advantage.
4. Use it sparingly. Don't touch if possible. Tap savings only for truly rainy days, unexpected expenditures, and genuine financial emergencies. Don't spend savings on regular bills and living expenses, shopping binges or luxury items.
5. If you must dip into your savings, replenish as soon as possible.
6. Watch God bless your store! Your savings account will grow if you will be faithful to contribute to it.

Money can't save itself; people must save it!

## A Word About Investing Money

Money can make money. People can prosper by wisely and prudently investing their financial resources. To invest means to commit money to something in order to earn a financial return. The purpose of making an investment is to use your money to gain more money. Investing illustrates the principle of return. We give something in order to gain something. We invest money to make money.

> To *invest* means to commit money to something in order to earn a financial return. The purpose of making an investment is to use your money to gain more money.

The parable of the talents in Matthew 25:14-30 illustrates the practice of investing. The men with five talents and two talents "traded" and "gained," doubling their talents. They were commended and rewarded handsomely by their master. The man with one talent buried it. He didn't invest, nor did he gain. He was scolded and punished for his poor stewardship of his master's money.

The lessons of the parable of the talents are summed up in verses 21 and 29.

> *His master said to him, "Well done good and faithful slave; you were faithful with a few things, I will put you in charge of many things, enter into the joy of your master."*
> — Matthew 25:21

*To everyone who has shall more be given, and he shall have an abundance; but from the one who does not have, even what he does have shall be taken away.*
— Matthew 25:29

God gives more to those who make the most of what they have.

God gives more to those who make the most of what they have.

## Practical Pointers on Investing Money

1. Invest money you can live without. Begin with a small sum of discretionary income. Be conservative. Remember, it's the Lord's money. Low risk investing is the place to start.
2. Invest for the long haul. Avoid "get rich quick" schemes. Proverbs 28:20 says a faithful man will abound with blessing, but he who makes haste to be rich will not go unpunished.
3. Invest with reputable people and companies. Make sure your conscience is clear concerning your investment relationships.
4. Commit investments to prayer and God's direction.

# Life Insurance, Wills, and Inheritances:
## What Do They Have to Do With Financial Stewardship?

Lifestyle stewardship is a long-term commitment. Servanthood and stewardship occur over an entire lifetime. Monetary faithfulness means taking care of the financial business that God entrusts to us from the beginning to the very end of our earthly sojourn. We must properly manage, carefully protect, and wisely distribute material resources and financial assets that God provides to us.

Appropriate life insurance coverage protects our accumulated resources for those we leave behind. If a Christian's death wipes out all his resources and leaves his dependents destitute, what kind of stewardship is that? It is a biblical responsibility to make reasonable plans for the provision of your family and God's work while you are alive and when you die. The type, the amount of coverage, and the length of coverage is an individual decision that must be made through prayer and consultation with a qualified financial planner.

Eight out ten Americans do not have a written will. Therefore, when they die, the state or someone else, not them, will decide and dictate what happens to their assets. Proverbs 13:2 states that a good man leaves an inheritance to his children's children, and the wealth of the sinner is stored up for the righteous.

This verse tells us that the world's wealth will come to God's people and a good (righteous or godly) man leaves an inheritance to his family members. If wealth is put in our hands to be passed on to the following generations, it only makes sense that we make the decisions regarding the disposition of our money and material assets.

The good, or righteous, man thinks and plans ahead. He arranges to leave a legacy to his children and grandchildren. This legacy, or inheritance, is multifaceted: spiritual, moral, family/relational, material, and financial. How can a good man leave a legacy to his family if he has no power to distribute what he possesses because he didn't have a written will in place?

Even in death a believer, not an unbelieving world, should be the one who decides the disposition of his money and material resources. Christians should make it very clear in their last will and testament to whom and where their God-given resources go upon their homegoing. As managers of Kingdom resources, we must be faithful to the end. Anything less is poor stewardship.

Do you have a written will on file with your attorney? If you do, is it up-to-date and current? If not, rectify this situation right away. A will is not expensive in light of the overall investment you are making as a faithful manager of God's money and material resources. Don't delay. Take some time, spend some money, and write a will.

## Managing Material Resources

From the time they were young, I have taught my children this simple principle: If you want something bigger or better tomorrow than what you have today, take excellent care of what you have now. This truth is based on the spiritual law we studied in Luke 16:10, which says: He who is faithful in a very little thing is faithful also in much....

We each possess material assets (property, houses, automobiles, clothing, furniture, personal computers, athletic equipment, etc.). Faithfully managing these assets means keeping things in tiptop shape, good running order, presentable, and protected. It also means laboring to increase their value where we can because they are in excellent condition.

> If you want something bigger or better tomorrow than what you have today, take excellent care of what you have now.

Material things last longer and perform, or serve us, better when they are properly maintained. Good stewardship of what we have sets the stage for receiving even greater blessings from God.

Do you have a history of taking good care of what you have? Could God trust you with more because you have been faithful to take care of less? Good stewards are thankful for what they have and show that gratitude to God by taking excellent care of what they have received.

> Good stewards are thankful for what they have and show that gratitude to God by taking excellent care of what they have received.

## Check Your Checkbook

You can tell a lot about a person's priorities by examining how they spend their time and money. Checkbook registers, or ledgers, give an accurate reflection and financial record of how most people manage their money. Checkbooks don't lie!

If you want to see if you are managing God's money faithfully, apply the following criterion to your checkbook:

1. Does your register show entries for tithe (a full ten percent of your income) checks written to your local church?
2. What about checks for offerings and special gifts to God's work?
3. What does it reveal concerning assistance for the poor? Have you given any money given to Christian rescue missions, food pantries, clothing outlets, shelters for the homeless, etc? Contributed money or goods to organizations that reach out to the poor in your community?
4. Do you pay your regular monthly bills in full and on time? Your taxes?
5. How much of your income is going to cover debt service on credit cards, mortgages, or to other lenders? Is your debt load reasonable and manageable? Does your debt load need to be re-evaluated?
6. What about savings and investments? Is any money being deposited into a savings account, even a small amount on a consistent basis?
7. Have you planned to set aside some money for your last will and testament?

Mature people manage their money well.

> *God is able to make all grace abound to you, that always having all sufficiency in everything, you may have an abundance for every good deed.*
> — 2 Corinthians 9:8

# Lesson 13

## Managing Your Testimony

*You shall receive power when the Holy Spirit has come upon you; and you shall be My witnesses, both in Jerusalem, and in all Judea and Samaria, and even to the remotest part of the earth.*
*— Acts 1:8*

*Peter and John answered them and said, "Whether it is right in the sight of God to heed to you rather than to God, you be the judge; for we cannot stop speaking what we have seen and heard."*
*— Acts 4:19-20*

### PRINCIPLES
- Every Christian has a story to tell that needs to be told.
- God entrusts us with the work of witnessing to a lost world.
- Faithful stewards share their faith through lifestyle evangelism.

### PURPOSE
If you are a Christian, Jesus Christ has changed your life.

The purpose of this lesson is simple and straightforward: to realize that it is our responsibility as God's stewards to share our story of salvation with the lost.

As His witnesses, we give testimony of how the Lord has saved us from hell by forgiving our sins, and how He secured us for heaven by graciously giving us the free gift of eternal life. Born-again Christians are appointed and anointed to faithfully manage the message of salvation. We are commanded, and held accountable, to give witness of our new life in Him to those who need the Lord. As Good News bearers, our most important business is the business of witnessing and winning souls.

Dawson Trotman said, "Soul-winners are not soul-winners because of what they know, but because of Whom they know, how well they know Him, and how much they long for others to know Him." The most effective way for born-again believers to reach unbelievers for the Kingdom of God is through lifestyle evangelism — living the life of Christ before people on a daily basis.

Successful stewards are serious about being faithful to share their faith.

> It is our responsibility as God's stewards to share our story of salvation with the lost.

## DISCUSSION

Dwight L. Moody was one of the most effective Christian evangelists the world has ever known. His ministry was centered in Chicago in the late 1800's and early 1900's. His dynamic influence and soul-winning effectiveness ultimately spread around the world.

One night Moody was walking home when he saw a man leaning against a lamppost. Stepping up to the stranger and placing his hands upon his shoulders, the evangelist bluntly asked, "Sir, are you a Christian?" The man flew into a rage, doubled up his fist, and it seemed for a moment that Mr. Moody might be in serious trouble. "I'm sorry if I have offended you," he said quietly. "Why don't you mind your own business!" roared the man. "You must be D.L. Moody."

Moody's reputation for soul-winning preceded him. The evangelist made it his business to share his faith with people wherever he went. Why? Two reasons. First, Jesus Christ had radically changed D.L.Moody's life when he was born-again. Second, soul-winning was Moody's business because it was his Savior's business. In Luke 19:10, Jesus clearly stated His primary purpose in coming to earth: The Son of Man has come to seek and to save that which was lost.

The Lord's mission was to seek out lost people and bring them to a saving knowledge of God. As "the way, the truth, and the life..." (John 14:6), Jesus' sacrificial death on the Cross and His subsequent resurrection made it possible for people to be saved. Just before He ascended to heaven, having accomplished His earthly mission, Jesus commissioned the Church to go into all the world and make disciples (followers) (Matthew 28:18-20, Mark 16:15, Luke 9:1-2, 60, and Acts 1:8). The Church's high and holy purpose was to seek out and win the lost in His name. It still is!

In his book, *Say It With Love*, author Howard Hendricks makes an astute observation concerning the New Testament church: "Did it ever occur to you as you read through the New Testament that there is a remarkable absence of exhortation to share your faith? I don't think it occurred to the early church not to share their faith. The rank and file Christians were going everywhere witnessing." Personal and corporate witnessing for Christ was woven into the fabric of the first Christians' everyday life. The undeniable pattern of the early church was boldly and effectively witnessing for Christ.

> The undeniable pattern of the early church was boldly and effectively witnessing for Christ.

Read for yourself the following Scriptures in the book of Acts concerning how the New Testament church witnessed to its world:

Chapters 2:14-36; 3:6, 11-26; 4:7-33; 5:17-21, 29-32; 7; 8:4-40; 9:20-22; 10:34-48; 13:1-5, 16-43; 16:22-34; 17:1-6, 16-41; 18:1-5; 22:1-5; all of chapters 24 and 26; and 28:22-28.

Our Christian ancestors were passionate and persuasive in sharing their faith. They knew nothing else. Our first generation brothers and sisters in Christ were soul-winners from the beginning. There was no need for them to run off to evangelism conferences to get fired-up about soul-winning; they were fired-up, lifestyle evangelists who witnessed to people with the power of the Holy Spirit as a natural part of their Christian life. The testimony of a changed life flowed out of their hearts into everyday living, touching everyone they had the opportunity to influence.

## What About Witnessing Today?

Church-growth surveys over the last fifty years consistently report that only five percent of professing Christians in the United States have ever shared their personal faith with someone else. That's five out of one hundred! With this in mind, is it any wonder that most churches show little or no growth year after year? Should we be surprised that our nation is mired in the muck of a self-destructive spiritual and moral decline?

In many quarters Christianity has lost its influence and impact. As the salt of the earth we have become flavorless and as the light of the world (Matthew 5:12-13) our once bright-shining Gospel light is dim and dull. We have drifted far from the New Testament pattern for positively penetrating a culture for Christ.

The early church behaved quite differently. Acts 17:6 KJV records a thought-provoking statement about the New Testament church and its spiritual and moral impact on its culture: *These that have turned the world upside down are come hither also.* The disciples were marked men. People took notice of who they were and what they did. As Christ's witnesses, they made a startling difference in their world. For God and for good, they literally upset their world by turning a godless, upside-down society right side up!

That cannot be said of the modern day church. With shocking statistics like these, it is alarmingly apparent that an astonishing ninety-five out of every one hundred believers have no serious understanding of stewardship of the Gospel. Christ's business, winning souls, is clearly not their business.

How do you feel about the fact that only five percent of Christians ever share their faith with anybody? Does it matter to you?

Our Christian ancestors were passionate and persuasive in sharing their faith. They knew nothing else. Our first generation brothers and sisters in Christ were soul-winners from the beginning.

# God's Witnesses to the World

A witness is someone who tells another person what he has seen or heard. If you were standing on a street corner and saw two automobiles crash into one another at the intersection, a police officer investigating the accident might ask you to give testimony as to what you saw and heard. As an eyewitness of the event, you simply report what you see.

In Acts 1:8 Jesus said to His disciples "You shall be My witnesses." Note whose witnesses Christ said His followers would be. The disciples were not witnesses for themselves. They were witnesses for God. A Christian witness testifies what God has done for them. Lorne Sanny said, "Witnessing is taking a good look at the Lord Jesus Christ and telling others what you have seen."

The word *martus* translated "witness" is used thirteen times in the New Testament. The Greek root word denotes one who can or does confidently assert what he has seen or heard or knows. A witness is one who tells what he has seen, heard and knows. Our English word *martyr* comes from *martus*. It's a powerful word. A martyr is one who bears witness by his death. Witnessing for God is sacred and serious business. Christ's witnesses not only testify about what God has done in and for them, but they are also willing to lay their lives down for their testimony.

## The First Christian Witnesses

In Acts 4:1-33 we read the record of the first witnessing incident of the early church. Acts 3, gives the account of a mighty healing miracle that had taken place. A forty-year-old man, lame from birth, was begging at the Temple entrance. Peter said to the paralyzed man, "In the name of Jesus Christ the Nazarene — walk!" (Acts 3:6). Immediately, the man leaped to his feet and walked! He ran into the Temple, rejoicing! His transition from lame to leaping provided a literal "walking witness," or testimony of what God had done for him.

The community was shocked. Some believed and glorified God. Others didn't. The disciples were taken to task by the religious and legal authorities. They were arrested and put in prison. What was the charge? The disciples were incarcerated for preaching that Jesus was risen from the dead (Acts 4:1-3) and that by His name the lame man was healed (Acts 3:15-16, 4:10).

> A witness is someone who tells another person what he has seen or heard. If you were standing on a street corner and saw two automobiles crash into one another at the intersection, a police officer investigating the accident might ask you to give testimony as to what you saw and heard.

The religious authorities were unpleasantly surprised by what had happened. They had to confess that a truly noteworthy miracle had taken place through them (the disciples) and it was apparent to all who live in Jerusalem (Acts 4:16). Powerless to deny what had happened, they attempted to stop the spread of the Christian message. They wanted to stamp it out like an infectious disease! They threatened the disciples and commanded them not to speak or teach in Jesus' name anymore (Acts 4:17-18).

But Peter and John responded to their threats with conviction and boldness. "Whether it is right in the sight of God to give heed to you rather than God, you be the judge; for we cannot stop speaking what we have seen and heard." (Acts 4:19-20). The disciples rejected the religious authorities' position and obvious political power play. They challenged them to make up their minds whether people should listen to God or men.

Peter and John had already made up their minds. Jesus said, "You shall be My witnesses...." They were and they did. They could not and would not stop testifying about God's work in their lives.

The disciples did not stop speaking about what they had seen and heard. Their lives were threatened, but it didn't matter. Acts 4:24-31 says they took the threats to the Lord in prayer, asked for greater boldness, and received it through the infilling of the Holy Spirit. Intimidation didn't prevent them from declaring what they knew about faith in the Lord Jesus Christ. They were completely committed to being witnesses for Jesus Christ in their world.

Acts 4:33 says of these first Christian witnesses: "With great power the apostles were giving witness to the resurrection of the Lord Jesus, and abundant grace was upon them all." Great power and abundant grace were the benefits and blessings of being faithful witnesses for Christ.

Those in the early church were completely committed to being witnesses for Jesus Christ in their world. Their record of testifying about Jesus provides a perfect example of lifestyle evangelism for every Christian generation.

## Witnessing in Your World

You are responsible and accountable to give witness to your generation of your saving relationship with God through Jesus Christ. Your world needs to hear your salvation story.

> The disciples rejected the religious authorities' position and obvious political power play. They challenged them to make up their minds whether people should listen to God or men.

Acts 1:8 contains three principles concerning Christian witnessing:

*You shall receive power when the Holy Spirit has come upon you, and you shall be My witnesses, both in Jerusalem, and in all Judea and Samaria, and even to the remotest part of the earth.*

## Christians Are Witnesses by the Command of God

The church received her marching orders from her commander-in-chief when Jesus said, "You shall be My witnesses." Note that witnessing was not a suggestion; it was a command. In the context preceding verse 8, Acts 1:2 says, "Until the day He was taken up, after He had by the Holy Spirit given orders to the apostles whom He had chosen" and Acts 1:4 states "And gathering them together, He commanded them not to leave Jerusalem, but to wait for what the Father had promised."

The words *orders*, *commanded*, and *shall* are directive words. Witnessing is not optional for Christians. We are commanded and ordered to be His witnesses in our world. From our closest circle (Jerusalem) to the widest (remotest parts of the earth) we are commanded to be His witnesses.

Commands from God are to be obeyed and followed. A Christian who is not being an active witness for Christ is being disobedient to God.

Read Acts 26:19-29. This witnessing incident took place near the end of Paul's ministry before the Roman King Agrippa.

> Witnessing is not optional for Christians. We are commanded and ordered to be His witnesses in our world.

1. Was Paul obedient or disobedient to the vision God gave him?

   _____

2. According to verse 22, with God's help, Paul stood before great and small men doing what?

   _____

   _____

   _____

3. What was the content of Paul's preaching or testimony before men?

   _____

   _____

   _____

   _____

4. What effect did Paul's testimony have on King Agrippa? (v. 28).

_____

_____

_____

_____

5. What did Paul hope would happen soon to the king? (v. 29).

_____

_____

_____

_____

_____

Throughout his entire life and ministry, Paul witnessed for Christ. Ananias, led by the Holy Spirit, told Paul immediately following Paul's conversion "You will be a witness for Him to all men of what you have seen and heard" (Acts 22:15). Paul was God's witness.

The apostle of grace was effective. God always assisted him in witnessing to men because he was obedient to God's command and call to witness for the Lord.

## Christians Are Witnesses by the Power of God

Not only does God enlist and command His followers to be His witnesses, He also empowers them to be successful. When a military commander orders his troops into combat, he supplies them with the weaponry and firepower they need to take their objective. Before the disciples began witnessing, they waited for the power of the Holy Spirit to come upon them. Their spiritual firepower for witnessing came from God, not themselves.

The word translated *power* in Acts 1:8 is the Greek word *dunamis*. We derive our word dynamite from *dunamis*. Dynamite is powerful. Its explosive energy rearranges things in a hurry! Biblically, dunamis is supernatural power or energy that God provides to get the witnessing job done. It's critical to take note of the divinely ordered sequence of events stated here. Jesus said, "You shall receive power when the Holy Spirit has come upon you and (then) you shall be My witnesses...."

The Lord's command was twofold: Wait for power (verse 4), then witness for Me (verse 8). God's formula for successful soul winning is receive power first; witness second. Power must always precede witnessing. Before they went witnessing, the disciples had to wait for power.

The apostle of grace was effective. God always assisted him in witnessing to men because he was obedient to God's command and call to witness for the Lord.

Supernatural power must be supplied and operating before we can be effective evangelists. Spiritual dynamite (dunamis) is received as a gift through the person of the Holy Spirit. The Holy Spirit Himself energizes and empowers believers to be effective witnesses.

## Spirit-filled Witnesses

Spiritual power for witnessing was promised by the Father and provided through the baptism of the Holy Spirit.

> As for me (John the Baptist), I baptize you with water for repentance; but He who is coming after me is mightier than I, and I am not fit to remove His sandals; He will baptize you with the Holy Spirit and fire.
> — Matthew 3:11

> On the last day, the great day of the feast, Jesus stood and cried out, saying, "If any man is thirsty, let him come to Me and drink. He who believes in Me, as the Scripture said, "From his innermost being shall flow rivers of living water. But this He spoke of the Spirit whom those who believed in Him were to receive; for the Spirit was not yet given, because Jesus was not yet glorified.
> — John 7:37-39

> Then He opened their minds to understand the Scriptures, and He said to them, "Thus it is written, that Christ should suffer and rise again from the dead the third day; and that repentance for forgiveness of sins should be proclaimed in His name to all the nations, beginning from Jerusalem. You are witnesses of these things. And behold, I am sending forth the promise of My Father upon you; but you are to stay in the city until you are clothed with power from on high.
> — Luke 24:45-49

Spiritual power for witnessing was promised by the Father and provided through the baptism of the Holy Spirit.

Before the disciples went out into the harvest field to testify of their faith, they were told to wait in an upper room in Jerusalem. They were not to leave until they were baptized with the Holy Spirit. The disciples did what God told them to do. They waited patiently and prayerfully for ten days. Acts 2:1-4 records the supernatural outpouring and infilling of the Spirit at Pentecost.

While they were waiting for the promise of the Father, supernatural signs and wonders from heaven suddenly flooded the room and they were all filled with the Holy Spirit. The fire of God fell as God promised, purifying and empowering each one to walk in the power of the Spirit and be effective witnesses for Him. The church was Spirit-filled and ready for witnessing!

## SPIRIT-FILLED WITNESSING

Review Acts 2:32-33, 4:8, 4: 31 and 33, 5:3, 7:55, 11:24, 13:9, and 13:52, and 1 Corinthians 2:4. In all of these witnessing instances, the common denominator was being filled with the Holy Spirit!

## SUMMARY

Power and obedience are connected to one another. When we obey, we experience the power of God though the Holy Spirit.

> We are witnesses of these things; and so is the Holy Spirit, whom God has given to those who obey Him.
> — Acts 5:32

1. Have you obeyed God by receiving and being filled with the Holy Spirit according to Acts 2:1-4?

   _____

   _____

   _____

   _____

   _____

2. Are you obeying the Lord by actively witnessing for Him in the power of the Holy Spirit?

   _____

   _____

   _____

   _____

   _____

Power and obedience are connected to one another. When we obey, we experience the power of God though the Holy Spirit.

## Christians Are Witnesses of a Life Changed by God

Every Christian has a miraculous story of salvation and redemption to tell. Their life has been changed by the grace of God. The whole basis and bottom line of our Christian testimony is that we are different. God has changed our lives. Being born again, we aren't the same people we used to be; we don't do the same things we used to do. We have received new life in Christ!

Our testimony is an expression of the change that Jesus has brought to us. John 9 records the testimony of a blind man whose life was changed by Jesus. Responding to the religious bigots of the day who were accusing Jesus of being a sinner, this grateful man who had received his sight declared "Whether He is a sinner, I do not know; one thing I do know, that, whereas I was blind, now I see (John 9:25). The healed man's point: You theologians figure out if Jesus is a sinner or not; all I know and care about is that I am no longer sightless. I see because Jesus touched me and restored my sight!

There's power in a changed life. Look up the verses listed below and write down the changes that took place in the believer's life.

*Our testimony is an expression of the change that Jesus has brought to us.*

| VERSE | CHANGE |
|---|---|
| Ezekiel 36:26-28 | _____ |
| John 5:24 | _____ |
| Romans 6:4-5 | _____ |
| Romans 8:11, 14-17 | _____ |
| 2 Corinthians 5:17 | _____ |
| Galatians 6:15 | _____ |
| Ephesians 2:4-7 | _____ |
| Ephesians 4:24 | _____ |
| Colossians 3:10 | _____ |
| 1 Peter 2:9-10 | _____ |

## PERSONAL REFLECTION

1. How has your life changed since you received Christ as your personal Savior and Lord?

   _____

   _____

   _____

   _____

   _____

   _____

2. Who have you told recently about your new life in Christ?

   _____

   _____

   _____

   _____

   _____

*I am not ashamed of the Gospel, for it is the power of God for salvation to everyone who believes, to the Jew first and also to the Greek.*
— Romans 1:16

# Lifestyle Evangelism

God hasn't made many of us lawyers, but he has subpoenaed all of us as witnesses. We witness by what we say and what we do. Words and deeds. Speaking and serving. Lips and lifestyle. Both are important components of sharing our faith.

Being who you are is as important as what you say. In his book *Lifestyle Evangelism*, Joseph Aldrich writes "Our problem in evangelism is not that we don't have enough information — it is that we don't know how to be ourselves. We forget that we are called to be witnesses to what we have seen and known, not to what we don't know."

The most effective evangelism flows out of the everyday lifestyle of a Christian. We tell people what we know in the context of our daily living. Lifestyle evangelism focuses on relationships. We share what we know about Christ with the people in our circles of influence. Witnessing for Christ as a lifestyle should be as natural as breathing.

John 4 provides a classic example of lifestyle and relationship evangelism in action. Notice the natural progression of Jesus' evangelistic conversation that led to the conversion of the Samaritan woman at Jacob's well.

### Witnessing to a Woman at a Well

| | |
|---|---|
| Everyday situation | Sitting by the well vs. 1-6 |
| Casual conversation | Give me a drink vs. 7-8 |
| Breaking down barriers | You a Jew, I a Samaritan vs. 9-12 |
| Compassion for the woman | This water — eternal life vs. 13-15 |
| Caring Confrontation | Call your husband vs. 16-18 |
| Open communication | I perceive you are a prophet vs. 19-20 |
| Inspirational instruction | True worshippers vs. 21-26 |
| Influence and Impact | Come see a man vs. 27-20 |

The Lord Jesus, in an ordinary situation, built a relationship with a needy woman. That relationship resulted in her receiving living water (Christ) in her life. She then told others (witnessed) who also came to see Him. Lifestyle evangelism is sharing your faith in everyday life.

Being a witness for Jesus Christ is not something you do; it is who you are.

We witness by what we say and what we do. Words and deeds. Speaking and serving. Lips and lifestyle. Both are important components of sharing our faith.

## The Power of a Personal Story: Managing Your Testimony

A changed life has to be reckoned with. People may argue with theology, but they actually listen and pay careful attention to a personal testimony of a changed life. Dictionaries tell us the word *testify* means "to make a statement based on personal knowledge or belief; bear witness, to serve as evidence or proof; to attest; to show; to express and make known a personal conviction." Witnessing for Christ is testifying, or bearing witness, to the difference He has made in your life.

One of the simplest, most effective tools you can possess for sharing your faith is a written personal testimony. Putting your personal story of salvation on paper is a spiritual exercise that will pay untold dividends all the days of your life. Writing out your testimony will give you confidence when witnessing to your unsaved friends and acquaintances.

### Guidelines for a Written Testimony

You should be able to share your personal testimony in three minutes or less. Take a single sheet of paper and divide it into the three sections below. Prayerfully and thoughtfully write out your story according to this three-point outline. Your story should be interesting. Be honest. Keep to the facts. Make it clear and simple. Share at least one key Scripture. Commit what you write to memory.

> Evangelism is expressing what I possess in Christ and explaining how you can possess it too.
> —*Joseph Aldrich*

1. LIFE BEFORE CHRIST
   Significant facts, observations, and feelings about your life without Christ
2. HOW I RECEIVED CHRIST
   Share the actual steps you took to ask Jesus into your heart. List the who, what, where, when, and how information here.
3. LIFE AFTER CHRIST
   Highlight what your life is now like as a Christian. How Christ has changed your life. Share why you are so glad to be saved and on your way to heaven.

Practice sharing your personal testimony with fellow Christians. Let them help you fine tune your testimony before you share it with a non-Christian.

Being a witness for Jesus Christ is not something you do; it is who you are.

You should be able to share your personal testimony in three minutes or less.

210

## Helpful Suggestions for Sharing Your Faith Effectively

1. Ask the Lord for a soul-winner's heart. (See Matthew 9:35-38, Psalm 126, Proverbs 11:30).

2. Build a prospect list of unsaved people you have a positive relationship with.

3. Pray for your prospects regularly and look for an opportunity to witness.

4. Share your written personal testimony with them.

5. Serve your unsaved friends.

6. Sharpen your soul-winning skills:

   • Attend a soul-winning church.

   • Take a soul-winning course.

   • Read soul-winning material.

   • Learn from a proven personal soul-winner.

   • Familiarize yourself with "The Four Spiritual Laws" booklet by Campus Crusade for Christ.

   • Mark your Bible and memorize a simple soul-winning plan like the Modified Romans Road.

| | |
|---|---|
| God's love | John 3:16 |
| Man's sin | Romans 3:10, 23, |
| Christ's sacrifice | Romans 5:8 |
| Eternal life | Romans 6:23 |
| Repent | Acts 17:30 |
| Believe | Romans 10:13, John 1:12 |
| Confess | Romans 10:9-10 |
| Receive | Revelation 3:20 |

Servants and stewards. Christ's servants are stewards, or managers, of the Good News of Jesus Christ (the mysteries of God).

# Stewards of the Good News

The scriptural basis for this entire study has been 1 Corinthians 4:1-2 where Paul says, *"Let a man regard us in this manner as servants of Christ and stewards of the mysteries of God. In this case, moreover, it is required of stewards that one be found trustworthy."*

Servants and stewards. Christ's servants are stewards or managers of the Good News of Jesus Christ (the mysteries of God).

What do the following scriptures say about being stewards of the Gospel?

1 Corinthians 9:17-23 _____

Galatians 2:7_____

Colossians 1:25 _____

1 Thessalonians 2:4_____

1 Timothy 1:11_____

1 Titus 1:3_____


Your conclusion:

_____

_____

_____

_____

_____

_____

_____

_____

_____

The highest rung on the stewardship ladder is managing our testimony in a faithful manner through effectively witnessing to others about what Jesus has done for us.

We are required to be faithful in managing the message of salvation. God trusts us with the proclamation of the Good News! It is our responsibility to be found trustworthy of that trust. The Word of God that has power to change a person's destiny from hell to heaven is entrusted to our care. We cannot separate sharing the Gospel from our stewardship of God's resources.

The highest rung on the stewardship ladder is managing our testimony in a faithful manner through effectively witnessing to others about what Jesus has done for us.

Someone once said, "If your Christianity is worth having, it should be worth sharing." I respect and admire what Dr. Robert H. Schuller, pastor of the Crystal Cathedral in Orange County, California remarked about his church's mission: "I work as if our church were the only church of Jesus Christ in Orange County and the salvation of all the souls depended on us alone." This successful, influential church leader understands that Christians are God's channel for spreading the Good News. Like the New Testament church, he has the heart of a soul-winner. Dr. Schuller takes seriously the responsibility of a steward who desires to be found faithful in the management of the Gospel message.

## SUMMARY

Christians are managers of the Good News. Whether we are found faithful or unfaithful in this world-changing task is up to us!

## FOR FURTHER STUDY

The Word on witnesses, witnessing, and testifying in the Bible. Psalm 66:16, 75:15, 119:13, 46; Isaiah 43:10, 63:7; Jeremiah 20:29; Daniel 4:2; Jonah 1:9, John 1:15, 15:27; Acts 2:32; Mark 2:12, 5:15; John 9:8-9, 12:9; Acts 4:14, 16:32, Acts 26:22; 2 Corinthians 4:13, and 1 Peter 5:12.

THE GOSPEL ACCORDING TO YOU
You are writing a Gospel,
A chapter everyday.
By the things that you do,
And the words that you say.
Men read what you write,
Distorted or true;
What is the Gospel
According to you?
*The Christian Herald*

# Lesson 14

## Rewards of a Faithful Steward

*According to the grace of God which was given to me, as a wise master builder I laid a foundation, and another is building upon it. But let each man be careful how he builds upon it. For no man can lay a foundation other than the one which is laid, which is Jesus Christ. Now if any builds upon the foundation with gold, silver, precious stones, wood, hay and straw, each man's work will become evident; for the day will show it, because it is to be revealed by fire; and the fire itself will test the quality of each man's work. If any man's work which he has built upon it remains, he shall receive a reward.*
— 1 Corinthians 3:10-14

*His master said to him, Well done, good and faithful slave; you were faithful with a few things, I will put you in charge of many things; enter into the joy of your master.*
— Matthew 25:23

### PRINCIPLES
- Faithful stewards receive righteous rewards.
- God rewards faithful stewards in the here and now and the hereafter.

### PURPOSE
From cover to cover, the Bible promises rewards: negative rewards to evil, unfaithful people, and positive rewards to good, faithful people. Every person is rewarded according to the quality of belief, obedience, and service that marked their life on earth.

Our purpose in this final chapter is to tie up our study of lifestyle stewardship with the ribbon of biblical rewards. The Lord honors and richly rewards those who have been faithful in the management of His resources. We will discuss two types of positive rewards: temporal and eternal.

Faithful stewards can look forward to being rewarded both on earth and in heaven.

The Lord honors and richly rewards those who have been faithful in the management of His resources.

## DISCUSSION

A wealthy man went to visit his doctor. At the conclusion of an exhaustive battery of medical tests and physical examinations, his physician shared the findings with his patient. He told him that he had a terminal illness, and that his life would soon end. On the way home, he called a close friend and invited him out for a cup of coffee.

Telling his friend that he did not have much longer to live, he shared his feelings about life. "It's been deceiving," he said. "I have spent my whole life in getting rich. Now I have very little time left to enjoy or use my accumulated wealth."

It took a terminal illness for this man of means to realize, that in the long run, he had missed the meaning of life. Spending maximum time and energy on getting ahead, he devoted minimum effort in giving to others. Life's curtain was closing. There was no way to call back the years he had wasted in accumulating wealth. The real purpose of life had eluded him.

What accounts for the difference between insignificance or significance is not age, but attitude and action concerning servanthood and stewardship.

As John Maxwell said in a sermon on stewardship, "It's not the duration of life, but our donation to life that counts." When this rich man's life came to the end of the road (duration), he recognized that his service and stewardship (donation) to God and his fellow man had fallen short.

Making a lasting impact and influencing others is not about how many years you live, but what you do with your years. Some people may live to a ripe old age, but because they were consumers, their impact was negligible. Others may die young, but their influence was remarkable because they were contributors during their short lifespan. What accounts for the difference between insignificance or significance is not age, but attitude and action concerning servanthood and stewardship.

What we do with what we have while we have time to do it is the issue that really matters according to the Word of God. That's the essence of lifestyle stewardship.

## God Never Forgets Life's Donors!

As Christian stewards, we are donors to life. Our donations do not go unnoticed. It is possible that men may forget what we give and contribute throughout our lifetime. But God never will. The writer to the Hebrews reminded the Christians who were engaged in ministering to people that God never forgets what we do in His name.

*God is not unjust as to forget your work and the love which you have shown toward His name, in having ministered and in still ministering to the saints. And we desire that each one of you show the same diligence so as to realize the full assurance of hope until the end, that you may not be sluggish, but imitators of those who through faith and patience inherit the promises.*
— Hebrews 6:10-12

Because God never forgets what we have done and are currently doing, we can keep on doing Kingdom work with confidence. He is watching and making notes of our service and stewardship. Everything we do is recorded and eventually rewarded by the Lord.

Faithful stewards are not slow or sluggish about serving others. They remain diligent in their imitation of those who have gone before them, blazing a stewardship trail marked by faith and patience. Stewards who patiently trust until the end are the ones who have every hope to "inherit the promises" (receive the rewards).

> Faithful stewards are not slow or sluggish about serving others.

## PERSONAL REFLECTION

What comes to your mind when you see the word *reward*?

_____
_____
_____
_____
_____
_____
_____
_____
_____
_____

Think about a reward you have received. What did you do to earn it? Why was it so special to you?

_____
_____
_____
_____
_____
_____

Have you ever given a reward to someone else? How did you feel rewarding another person?

_____

_____

_____

_____

_____

_____

_____

Why do you think God rewards good people with good things?

_____

_____

_____

_____

_____

_____

Are you personally convinced that God remembers your service and will reward you for your faithfulness?

_____

_____

_____

_____

_____

The next time you serve the Lord and no one seems to notice or care, stand on Hebrews 6:10!

Paul gives scriptural guidelines in 1 Corinthians 3:10-14 for those servants and stewards of God who desire to receive a reward.

# The Biblical Basis of a Believer's Rewards

Describing himself as "a wise master builder according to the grace of God," Paul gives scriptural guidelines in 1 Corinthians 3:10-14 for those servants and stewards of God who desire to receive a reward. We can make at least seven observations from this passage.

**Observation One.** Jesus Christ is the only one true foundation on which to build spiritual works (v. 11).

Notice that no man can lay a foundation. It has already been laid down! God the Father, sent God the Son to the earth to die and be raised again for our sins.

Jesus is the foundation for salvation. There is no other foundation that anyone can lay. After being born-again through personal faith in Christ, believers "build" their Christian life upon the Lord.

**Observation Two.** Every believer must be careful about how he builds his life upon Christ (v. 10).

God has established a certain way for us to carry out our mission of faithful servanthood and stewardship. We must be on guard against carelessness in the way we build. Each believer's responsibility and duty is to watch how they build and with what kind of works they construct their spiritual house.

**Observation Three.** We can use two different types of materials to build our Christian lives (v. 12).

"Gold, silver, and precious stones" are one type. "Wood, hay, and stubble" are another. As builders of our lives, we determine which set of elements will be used in constructing our spiritual house. Each set of elements represents a different type of work for Christ.

**Observation Four.** The type of materials a man uses will be revealed by the test of fire (v. 13).

Our Christian works will be subjected to a trial by fire. This fire will reveal whether we built with perishable or imperishable materials.

**Observation Five.** The purpose of the "fire" is to reveal the quality of our work (v. 13).

The clear emphasis here is on quality, not quantity, of works. Size, volume, mass, or the popularity of a person or ministry doesn't impress God. The Lord looks for the motive, the reason why people do what they do.

Therefore, a widow with a couple of pennies (Luke 21:1-4) is highly esteemed, remembered, and rewarded by God because of the quality, not the quantity, of her sacrificial gift. When it comes to works, all believers, because of Christ, can build their spiritual life on a level playing field. Quality, not quantity, is the key criterion for Kingdom rewards.

**Observation Six.** Rewards are given to those whose works remain after being tested by fire (v. 14).

Each believer's responsibility and duty is to watch how they build and with what kind of works they construct their spiritual house.

It is obvious that works of "wood, hay, and stubble" will burn up. Works of "gold, silver, and precious stones" on the other hand, will not be consumed, but will be purified as they withstand the heat of God's inspection. Works of "wood, hay, and stubble" are incinerated by the fire, reduced to an ash heap — resulting in loss for the worker (v. 15). Persons whose works remain ("gold, silver, and precious stones") receive rewards.

**Observation Seven.** God is committed to giving rewards to those who build their lives on the right foundation with the right materials (v. 14).

Christians who build on Christ are wise (like the wise master builder Paul!) and will be richly rewarded. Good works, and deeds that flow from faithful servanthood and stewardship build a solid spiritual life that will stand for time and eternity.

## SUMMARY

Servanthood and stewardship are "gold, silver, and precious stones." Servants and stewards of Christ who are found faithful and trustworthy survive the fire of God that tests their works. Their works of service and management of God's resources remain. Servants and stewards receive God's richest rewards.

# Rewards on Earth

The largest part of a faithful steward's rewards are awarded in heaven. But those people who have been trustworthy to manage God's resources here on earth do not go without rewards while still living. In addition to the rewards for faithfulness discussed in Lesson 3, there are at least three other temporal rewards worth mentioning.

## Favor With God and Man

Favor is a benefit of the righteous person who lives faithfully according to the Word of God. The word *favor* means "friendly regard, to your advantage, in good graces with others, preferential treatment."

To have favor with people means that they show a favorable disposition toward you. They like you and do good to you. When you have favor, good things happen to you that don't happen to those who are in disfavor with the same person.

Favor gives God's people an edge, or an advantage, in working with this world.

Servanthood and stewardship are "gold, silver, and precious stones." Servants and stewards of Christ who are found faithful and trustworthy survive the fire of God that tests their works.

The Bible declares that the righteous man has favor (is in good graces and gets preferential treatment) with both God and man. Over eighty-seven references in the Word use some form of the word *favor* (i.e. favorable, favored) The source of favor is God. Psalm 5:12 declares that the righteous are surrounded with God granted favor:

> *It is Thou who dost bless the righteous man, O Lord, Thou dost surround*
> *him with favor as with a shield.*
> — Psalm 5:12

God surrounds the righteous with what I call a "favor shield." Those God declares righteous because of their relationship with Him through faith in His Son Jesus Christ are covered and protected with a shield of favor. This shield goes before them, providing a divine covering that ensures they will be on the receiving end of special treatment. Faithful servants and stewards of God are "blessed" with favor.

Special treatment comes from the Lord first. Why? Because of the righteous person's relationship with Him. My children always have favor with me because I am their daddy. I love other people's children; but they don't have favor with me the way my kids do! Our relationship as family is the foundation for favorable treatment.

Special, or favorable, treatment comes second, from man and this world. God makes sure that His people receive discounts and bargains on purchases, the best deals in business, connections, and networks to people who can assist us, raises in salaries, promotions, exceptional terms with banks, and so forth. Why? Because we are God's kids, and Father God looks out for His family members!

We have an advantage in this world because we belong to the Lord and live for another world!

## The World's Wealth Comes to Faithful Stewards

This temporal reward is often overlooked by believers — maybe because it seems too good to be true!

God's Word promises that the wealth of the world will come to the righteous.

> *Then you will see and be radiant, and your heart will thrill and rejoice;*
> *Because the abundance of the sea will be turned to you, the wealth of the*
> *nations will come to you.*
> —Isaiah 60:5

Favor gives God's people an edge, or an advantage, in working with this world. The Bible declares that the righteous man has favor (is in good graces and gets preferential treatment) with both God and man.

*The wealth of the sinner is stored up for the righteous.*
— Proverbs 13:22

Other Scriptures supporting this principle are found in Psalm 37:11, 22; Isaiah 57:13; Matthew 5:5; and Romans 4:13.

According to Proverbs 13:22, the unrighteous man ("sinner") stores up wealth (material and financial resources) that will eventually go to the righteous person. The worldly man opens a savings account for the godly, and he doesn't even know it! God transfers the wealth from the worldly man to the Kingdom person.

The Exodus of Israel from Egypt provides a scriptural example of this principle of transfer of wealth. Exodus 12:36 reads: "The Lord had given the people favor in the sight of the Egyptians, so that they let them have their request. Thus they plundered the Egyptians." In the verses preceding this verse, Moses asked Pharaoh's permission to lead God's people into the desert to worship the Lord. God granted Moses and Israel favor with the Egyptian leader. The result: Egypt's possessions were plundered by Israel.

Egypt, a symbol of the world system, financed Israel's exodus (the way out) from bondage to freedom! The wealth of Egypt was stored up for Israel. Former slaves, who for over four hundred years were extremely poor, suddenly found themselves rich and on their way to the Promised Land!

> The wealth of the world is stored up for the righteous because a) God's people are involved in a great cause and b) God can trust the righteous to use worldly riches in the proper manner.

The wealth of the world is stored up for the righteous because
a)  God's people are involved in a great cause, and
b)  God can trust the righteous to use worldly riches in the proper manner.

When we are faithful as stewards to give our worldly goods to God, God makes sure that the world's goods come to us. Who, what, where, when, how and how much, is up to God. His purpose and timing is always perfect.

This exciting promise from God, is a biblical fact and an earthly reward. The wealth of the sinner is stored up for the righteous.

## Personal Satisfaction from Being a Successful Steward

Last, but certainly not least, there is great satisfaction and joy in knowing that you have been faithful as God's servant and steward. Only the heart knows how good it feels to be rewarded for accomplishing what God has called us to do.

With confidence and a deep, abiding sense of inner satisfaction, Paul declared in 2 Timothy 4:7, "I have fought the good fight, I have finished the course, I have kept the faith." As Paul anticipated the crown of righteousness awaiting him in glory (verse 8), he could rest and be at peace that he had been faithful in his servanthood and stewardship.

There's nothing like knowing deep within that you have been faithful to God and what He has called you to do. Satisfaction with yourself before the Lord and men is an incomparable and immeasurable reward of the righteous.

# Rewards in Heaven

Heaven. The Christian's hope of an eternal home with the Lord Jesus Christ. A very special place, depicted as "many dwelling places in My Father's house" by Jesus in John 14:1-4. A place that the Lord is preparing for us, even now. He's getting everything ready for our homecoming. Jesus' sole purpose in preparing our heavenly home is so that we can be there with Him. Jesus promised the disciples, " I will come again and receive you to Myself, that where I am, there you may be also" (v. 3). Oh, what a happy day for all believers when Jesus returns to take us home to heaven!

Chuck Swindoll, in his excellent book *Improving Your Serve*, discusses the subject of heaven and what will happen there: "Even though the Bible is clear in declaring that there is a home prepared for us, and even though it is clear that that home is ours to claim for eternity, a lot of fuzzy thinking goes on regarding heaven. In fact, it is shrouded in mystery. If you question that, ask the average Christian you know what he thinks heaven is going to be like. You will get all sorts of answers."

Study the subject of heaven. Take a Bible concordance and look up the verses and passages on heaven. Then write in your own words what you think heaven will be like.

_____
_____
_____
_____
_____
_____
_____
_____
_____

> Satisfaction with yourself before the Lord and men is an incomparable and immeasurable reward of the righteous.

Whatever else may be said about heaven, according to the Bible it is a place of reward. Eternal blessings will be awarded to those who lived godly lives in the service of Christ on earth. A "well done" and numerous "crowns" await the faithful.

# Well Done

There is nothing like the words "well done" spoken over you when you have done well! We crave words of praise, approval, and commendation. Something inside us warms up and glows when someone we respect and admire notices and commends us for our accomplishments. Imagine when they come from Almighty God! It's one thing to have an earthly father commend you with a "well done," but it is quite another when your heavenly Father says, "Well done, my good and faithful servant."

Eternal blessings will be awarded to those who lived godly lives in the service of Christ on earth. A "well done" and numerous "crowns" await the faithful.

Study the parable of the talents in Matthew 25:14-30 again.

1. In verses 21 and 23, what phrase did the master use to praise the first two servants?

   _____
   _____
   _____

2. Why was the affirmation "Well done, good and faithful servant" conferred? What did the servants do?

   _____
   _____
   _____
   _____
   _____

3. How were the faithful servants rewarded by the master?

   _____
   _____
   _____
   _____
   _____
   _____

4. Why wasn't the third servant rewarded with a "well done"?

_____

_____

_____

_____

_____

5. What happens in your heart when you read the words "Well done, good and faithful servant, enter into the joy of your master"?

_____

_____

_____

_____

_____

6. Are you looking forward to this word of commendation from your Lord and Master?

_____

_____

_____

_____

7. How will you qualify for such a wonderful commendation?

_____

_____

_____

_____

Faithful servants of God will receive the incomparable praise ;"Well done" from the lips of Jesus. They will also be warmly welcomed to enjoy the presence of the Lord forever in glory!

# Crown Them With Many Crowns

Heaven is a place of celebration and coronation. Eternal crowns will be placed on the heads of those who prove themselves faithful in serving the Lord. The Bible reveals at least five crowns that are set aside for the Kingdom's faithful servants.

### The Imperishable Crown (1 Corinthians 9:24-27)
This reward goes to those who run life's race victoriously. Through personal

discipline and the power of the Holy Spirit, they keep their bodies under control, rising above their carnal appetites and desires to do what God has called them to do. This crown is promised to those who "run to win" and win their race.

How are you doing in running your race? (See Hebrews 12:1-2.) Are you winning your race? Will an imperishable crown be waiting for you?

### The Crown of Exultation (Philippians 4:1, 1 Thessalonians 2:19-20).

This is the soul-winners crown. This crown is a happy one. Paul speaks of two bodies of believers that are his joy and glory. He rejoices greatly in these converts. They will be his crown and reward in the presence of Jesus. There is a special crown that will be placed on the heads of those who win the lost to Christ.

Are you doing your part to win souls to Christ? Will you share in the coronation ceremony when the crown of exultation is given out?

> *Those who have insight (they that be wise) will shine brightly like the brightness of the expanse of heaven, and those who lead the many to righteousness (soul-winners) like the stars forever and ever.*
> — Daniel 12:3

### The Crown of Righteousness (2 Timothy 4:7-8)

This crown goes to those who are eagerly awaiting Jesus to return to take them home to heaven. These faithful folks "await and love His appearing" as Paul did. Like Paul in verse 7, they will confess with their mouths at the end of their earthly lives, "I have fought the good fight, I have finished the course, I have kept the faith...." Therefore, in the not-too-distant future a crown of righteousness is laid up for them. Note in verse 8, Paul says the Lord Himself ("the righteous Judge") will award this long-awaited and much anticipated crown.

Faithful believers will receive the crown of righteousness because they have been made the righteousness of God through their faith in Christ. (See Philippians 1:11, 3:9; and 2 Peter 1:1).

Are you fighting the good fight of faith each day as a servant of Christ and a trustworthy steward of the mysteries of God? How does your confession line up with Paul's in 2 Timothy 4:7? Are you eagerly awaiting, looking forward to by faith, and loving the thought of the Lord's appearing?

### The Crown of Life (James 1:12)

This crown is awarded to those saints who have suffered in a triumphant and noble manner as Christians.

Heaven is a place of celebration and coronation. Eternal crowns will be placed on the heads of those who prove themselves faithful in serving the Lord.

The recipients of this crown of life have not only "persevered under trial," they have loved Jesus every step along the path of tribulation and suffering. Because they loved the Lord, they endured and conquered, not giving up or giving in to the pressure of persecution and personal suffering. Love for Jesus that is proven through times of trial and suffering is rewarded by God.

The man who perseveres under trial is "blessed" and "promised by the Lord" the crown of life.

Does the way you handle life's trials make you a candidate for the crown of life as promised in James 1:12?

### The Crown of Glory (1 Peter 5:1-4)

This special reward is reserved for those who faithfully "shepherd the flock of God" entrusted to their care. They qualify for this crown because they willingly and humbly made sacrifices for the sheep, they lived exemplary lives — lives worth following.

Submitted to the Chief Shepherd while awaiting His glorious appearance, by serving the body of Christ these faithful undershepherds are promised the crown of glory.

If you are in a position of ministry, are you conducting your shepherding duties according to the above criteria? Would the sheep under your care say you deserve the crown of glory?

### SUMMARY

Sacred crowns are promised by God to those who are found faithful in serving the Lord and managing His resources. They are certainly worth working and waiting for!

> Faithful believers will receive the crown of righteousness because they have been made the righteousness of God through their faith in Christ.

> Sacred crowns are promised by God to those who are found faithful in serving the Lord and managing His resources. They are certainly worth working and waiting for!

# Crowns at His Feet

I can't think of a better way to close this chapter on the rewards of faithful stewards than to quote the Word on the greatest reward of all — worshipping and honoring our Lord and Savior Jesus Christ by casting our crowns at the holy feet of the one who alone is worthy to be crowned the King of kings and Lord of lords!

*When the living creatures give glory and honor and thanks to Him who sits on the throne, to Him who lives forever and ever, the twenty-four elders will fall down before Him who sits on the throne, and will worship Him who lives forever and ever, and will cast their crowns before the throne, saying, "Worthy art Thou, our Lord and our God, to receive glory and honor and power; for Thou didst create all things, and because of Thy will they existed, and were created."*

— Revelation 4:9-11

# Lesson 15

## Conclusion: Blessed to Be a Blessing!

Someone with excellent insight, and probably years of life experience, once observed that "real failure in life is failing to make the most of the gifts and resources God gives you."

The bottom line of lifestyle stewardship is this: God blesses us so we can bless others in His name. Everything we have studied and discussed in this book ends up at one logical conclusion. Servants and stewards of God are blessed so they can be a blessing to others.

That's The Trust.

Servants and stewards of God are blessed so they can be a blessing to others.

The very first covenant (sacred agreement) between God and man supports this principle of being blessed to be a blessing. Beginning with Abram, God established a high, holy, and happy purpose for His servants and stewards. God literally called Abram to leave his homeland and journey to a new land. There God promised Abram he would be blessed. Genesis 12:1-3 outlines Abram's call to be blessed and be a blessing to mankind.

> Now the Lord said to Abram, "Go forth from your country and from your relatives and from your father's house, to the land which I will show you. And I will make you a great nation, and I will bless you, and make your name great; And so you shall be a blessing; And I will bless those who bless you and the one who curses you I will curse. And in you all the families of the earth will be blessed."

Note all of the "I will's" referring to what God would do for Abram. God said He would lead him, make him a great nation, bless him, make his name great, bless those who blessed him, and curse those who cursed him. What a great deal for Abram! All he had to do was believe God. If he believed, he would be blessed.

But what was the reason for blessing Abram and his family? What purpose would blessing him so greatly serve? The families of the earth would be blessed too! "In you, Abram, all the families of the earth will be blessed. Through you, I will bring blessing to the entire earth. You Abram, as my servant and steward, will be My instrument to bring blessing to people everywhere!"

So what did Abram do regarding this mind-boggling offer? Verse 4 tells us Abram immediately packed up his family and belongings and obeyed God. Genesis 12-18 details Abram's (whose name God changed to Abraham in Genesis 17:5) incredible, inspiring faith journey.

Abraham believed God and it was counted to him as righteousness (See Romans 4:13-25.). As you trace Abraham's life until the day he died (Genesis 25:8) his spiritual legacy is a powerful testimony of accomplishing what God had called him to do: the Lord blessed Abraham and Abraham blessed others.

## Abraham, You, and Me

Through faith in Jesus Christ, Christians are spiritual descendants of Abraham. Our New Testament covenant with God, which is based on faith and grace, is even better than the one Abraham and the nation of Israel had under the law in the Old Testament. (See Hebrews 8-10.) It stands to reason that if Abraham was blessed to be a blessing, we who have a better covenant are blessed to be a blessing also!

God's people are not blessed just to be blessed. They are blessed in order to be a blessing!

## A Story of Stewardship

John and Matthew met through their sons' Little League baseball team. John, a minister, was in a season of transition. Unemployed for several months, he was waiting on the Lord for his next ministry assignment. Matthew owned a business that was struggling financially. He was the father of four children, three of them teenagers. His precious wife was battling cancer.

The men developed a close "iron sharpens iron" relationship. They shared their life situations on a regular basis, praying for each other and encouraging one another from the Word. As men who loved and served God, they looked to Him by faith to meet their needs.

Matthew and his family entered a very trying time. His wife went home to be with the Lord. His failing business went bankrupt. A worthless business partner left him with a pile of unpaid, back taxes owed to the IRS. Pressure and stress were mounting daily. It showed on Matthew's wearied and worried face.

God's people are not blessed just to be blessed. They are blessed in order to be a blessing!

It was a dark and difficult time for Matthew and his children. Besides grieving and adjusting to the loss of a wife and mother, the family fell on hard times financially. Making ends meet became a daily challenge.

One morning John was sitting in his living room planning a trip to the grocery store. His wife was working, so he did the shopping. He had a limited amount of money to spend, but as he drew up his list of items to purchase, he heard the Lord speak in his spirit.

Very clearly He said "I want to you take half of the money I have provided for you and buy groceries for Matthew and his kids. Spend the other half on your household. I also want you to take your children out of school early so they can shop with you. Take them with you to deliver the groceries. Give the food and supplies anonymously. Place the sacks on the porch, lay your hands on them and pray over them with your children, and then leave before Matthew comes home."

John sat quietly for a moment. In all honesty, he struggled with believing what he had heard. How could he buy groceries for Matthew when he had just enough money to purchase food for his own family? But he knew the voice of his heavenly Father. John told the Lord he would do just what He directed. John wrote two lists and headed out to pick his children up at school.

The children were ten and eight years old. When John shared with them what God had told them to do, the children were excited. The three of them talked about their "mission of mercy" on the way to the supermarket. Arriving at their destination, they grabbed two carts, and headed down the aisles, putting item after item into the rapidly-filling carts. More food went into Matthew's cart than into their own.

The purchases made, John and his children set out to make their delivery. Driving past Matthew's house, they spied out the land. When the coast looked clear, they pulled in, sprinting back and forth from car to house, until twelve bags of groceries were safe and secure on the front porch. Quickly, they put their hands on the bags, blessed the groceries, and prayed for God to prosper and watch over Matthew and his children. Then they ran to their car as fast as six feet could scoot!

Three days later, Matthew and John were sitting on the bleachers at a ballgame. Excitedly, Matthew leaned over to John and said, "John, I have to tell you what happened at our house a couple of days ago. You know I have been having a hard time paying the bills and getting groceries. Until the other day, I had always found a way to buy food for my family. But the other day the pantry hit rock bottom. All we had in the house was some bread, milk, and a few stale crackers. I didn't know what to say to the kids. My back was up against the wall. I saw no way out of our predicament.

"As I went to work, and the kids left for school, I called out to the Lord to show me how to feed my children.

"Would you believe I came home and found twelve grocery sacks full of food on our porch? I couldn't believe my eyes. No notes. Not a single trace of who might have done this. Just a bunch of good food to feed my kids. I wept over the bags and humbly thanked God for whoever blessed us. My kids were blown away by God's goodness in our time of need."

As Matthew related the story, John had to hold back his own tears. God used this opportunity to reassure an unemployed pastor and his family that God blesses all of us so we can bless others!

## Life Is Stewardship. Stewardship Is Life.

God is looking for people today who will decide to take what they have and allow it to be used by the Master. Our heavenly Father is looking for some consecrated lives (faithful stewards) through whom He can live out His principles and ministry. It was Dwight L. Moody who said, "The world has yet to see what God will do with and for and through and in and by the man or woman who is fully consecrated to Him."

What a challenge and invitation for each of us!

> *Let a man regard us in this manner, as servants of Christ, and stewards of the mysteries of God. In this case, it is required of stewards that one be found trustworthy.*
> — 1 Corinthians 4:1-2

God is looking for people today who will decide to take what they have and allow it to be used by the Master.

# WE WANT TO KNOW WHAT YOU THINK ABOUT THIS STUDY!

Please share your comments about this study by posting your review on our website. From the menu bar at the top of the Hensley Publishing home page, select **Our Products**. On the Products page, scroll down the page until you see the cover of the Bible study. Choose the study by clicking on the cover image. On the next screen, select **Write a Review** in the right column. Write your review and click on **Submit**.

You can see our complete line of Bible studies,
post a review, or order online and save at:

# www.hensleypublishing.com

# HENSLEY
PUBLISHING

6116 E 32nd St.
Tulsa, OK 74135

Toll Free Ordering: 800.288.8520
Fax: 918.664.8562
Phone: 918.664.8520

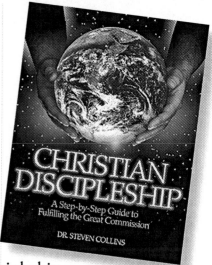

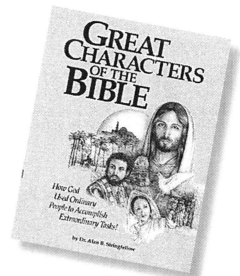

Printed in the United States
109209LV00003B/341-374/A

9 781563 220753